North Meadows

P9-ARU-551

The Wall

Pond

Cabin

Bridge

To The Deep
Unknown

KNOWN WORLD

reeg's
Quarry

N
W S E

Runt the Hunted

Runt the Hunted

Daniel Schwabauer

Clear Water Press
Olathe, Kansas

Runt the Hunted
by Daniel Schwabauer

Clear Water Press
PO Box 62
Olathe, KS 66051
www.clearwaterpress.com

Book design by CDS Creative Design
www.CDSCreativeDesign.com

Printed in the USA.

ISBN 978-09742972-3-1

Library of Congress Control Number: 2006906956

For Carrol

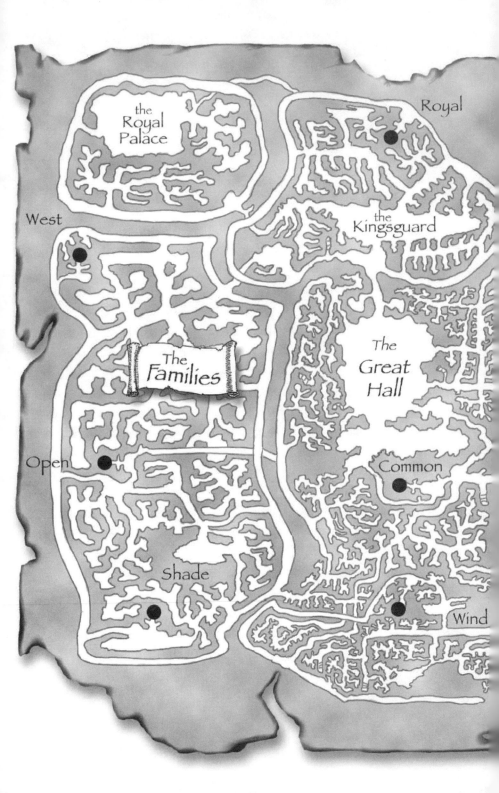

Pronunciation Guide

BlaKote - black odee

DeStra - dess truh

ElShua - el shoo uh

GoRec - go wreck

HaRed - ha red

JaRed - jare ed

JoHanan - joe han un

KahEesha - kaw ee shuh

KoVeek - ko veek

LaRish - la rish

Luk - luke

RahUlf - raw ulf

ReDemec - red uh mick

SoSheth - so sheth

TaMir - tuh meer

ThuBrik - thoo brick

Tira-nor - tier uh nor

Ur'Lugh - oor lug

YaGo - yah go

YuLooq - you luke

TaMir's Prophecy

In burrows deep through winter's sleep,
In tunnels cold as stone,
In damp, in gloom, in chamber-room,
Skin stretches over bone.

Kit and Mouse in mourning-house,
Lamenting Seer's doom,
Fear not fate; the claws of hate
Are carving out your tomb.

Split in two, the mad pursue
The weak: let city burn!
Hope will flee. Humility
Must face Lord Wroth's return.

In life, in death, at love's last breath,
When sounds the Badger's call;
The widow cries, a promise dies,
And Tira-Nor shall fall.

1

JaRed

They waited till after sunset to arrest him.

JaRed turned on his pallet as a familiar nightmare touched his spine. His body twitched. In the dream, faces stared at him through a curtain of fog, jaws stretching open.

"Heeah we ahhhh," a voice said.

He opened his eyes.

Claws circled his throat. His attacker pulled him out of the tiny sleeping space into the entry chamber of the ReDemec family home. Light from a glowstone exploded in his face, hovering on the outstretched paws of a huge mouse.

Mice ringed him, newcomers to the kingsguard, foreigners with elegant accents, their voices floating on too much air.

"Yes," whispered the one with eyes like fish eggs.

"Thaaat's him. Thaaat's JaRed. Son ahv ReDemec."
He offered a weak smile, eyelids drooping.

A fist smashed into JaRed's ribs, knocking the
breath out of him with a sound like a bellows. He fell
forward. His nose slammed into the anvil of a rising
knee.

White sparks curled in the darkness. Laughter.
Words he didn't understand, followed by a curse, clear
and unashamed.

A series of hammer blows crashed into his face,
someone's elbow rising and falling. Teetering, he
reached for the ground, but it lurched sideways and
slid beyond his grasp.

He groped, caught one of them by the ankle, and
twisted. It made an unpleasant sound. His victim
shrieked and fell, clutching at one leg.

"He still shows signs ahv life? RahUhlf?"

"Not for long, ThuBrik."

Lieutenant ThuBrik. The new officer from Cadrid.
JaRed's mind clutched at this information as though it
might save him, though he knew it meant nothing
good. These mice were part of the kingsguard now.
They wouldn't have attacked him without orders.

TaMir was right. *The king is going to kill me.*

Paws jerked him onto his back, tugged at his arms
and legs, stretched him into a taut, scarecrow X.

A new voice surprised them. "What are you doing?
Who are you? JaRed!" KahEeshah, JaRed's sister,

stepped into the light of the glowstone. Her sleep-heavy eyes widened. She screamed as one of the attackers clapped a paw across her mouth and shoved her against a wall.

"This one has been eating well," the mouse grunted. "Fat for a commoner."

"No!" ThuBrik said. "She is not to be harmed. Only him." He pointed at JaRed.

ReDemec, JaRed's father, stumbled into the chamber, his eyes lit with fire. It took two of them to restrain him. They failed to keep him quiet.

JaRed's older brother, HaRed, entered the chamber and stood frozen, watching. A blow to the back of his head knocked him to his knees.

Fists hooked under JaRed's armpits, the Cadridians yanked him upright.

"Take him to the Great Haahll."

They dragged him through the winding tunnels, his heels scraping shallow grooves in the earthen floor, his father's rage trailing after them.

Faces shot from other chamber holes along the corridor, then disappeared, curiosity stunted by fear. Old Grouser, his wire-brush eyebrows knotted. Gurgy, the fat digger who hauled for the engineers. SindHu, daughter of MarSihLu. Luk and Raz, the kits who played at war all winter, unbelief written on their faces. Whispers spread in his wake.

"JaRed Ratbane!"

"The war hero."

"The one who saved the city?"

"He's only a boy."

"Arrested? Why?"

"What has JaRed done wrong?"

He noticed, for the first time, the rough texture of the tunnel ceiling, how it cracked and pitted above the corridor. The expanse above the palace, where the king would be feasting on raisins even now, ran plaster-smooth.

What has JaRed done wrong? What does it matter? Right and wrong don't concern the king any more.

———&&&———

The beating continued when they reached the Great Hall. ThuBrik motioned for an end when the thugs who had restrained JaRed's father returned. RahUlhf gave JaRed a final exhausted kick and dragged him to the center of the massive chamber.

Pain racked JaRed's body. His tongue stuck to the roof of his mouth, dry as sand.

Mice from the Commons appeared in the tunnels. When no one drove them away, they inched closer. They were going to be allowed to watch. Some talked about JaRed as though he were already dead.

In an hour, the shadows near the walls of the Great Hall swelled with on-lookers. Words dribbled through the crowd—rumors, half-truths, speculations.

ONE

A voice in the back of his mind sang out, mocking him. *Too late to run, now! Too late! Too late!*

———∞∞∞———

He remembered the old seer, TaMir, huddling in one corner of his chamber, his white fur gray in the shadows. Immensely fat, his joints creaked when he moved. His knees mounded like boils under thinning fur, stiff and swollen with age. His eyes shone with intelligence.

"You must go soon," he said.

"Why?"

He grunted. "SoSheth will kill you if he can."

JaRed squinted into the darkness. TaMir's private chamber smelled like earth and moldering straw and the air after a rainstorm. "ElShua will protect me."

TaMir didn't answer.

"Won't he?"

"He will be ... with you."

JaRed stood. "Something terrible is coming, isn't it?"

TaMir's voice came like a long sigh, low and thin and full of weariness. "The king no longer serves ElShua. He no longer serves Tira-Nor. He serves only himself. And that is a dangerous lust, for the self is easily steered by Lord Wroth."

Wroth. The undying rat demon who—according to the stories—had brought evil into the world.

"What about the Commons? What about the kings-guard? Will they turn against me too?"

TaMir reached out, clutched JaRed's paw in his own. "If ElShua's promises looked possible," he said, his yellow teeth gnarled and dull in the darkness, "we wouldn't need them."

The royal prosecutor arrived; a tall thin mouse with gray fur and a cold, friendless face. ThuBrik saluted and retreated to one side, a picture of disciplined loyalty.

The prosecutor gazed at JaRed's prone form for a long moment. His nostrils flared, and he turned to look at the gathered mice. Silence descended, leeching down from the prairie overhead through the gloom-shrouded hill. "JaRed, son of ReDemec," he said, "You have been found guilty of sedition and treason."

A sound like rain spattered among the commoners, then evaporated.

"You plotted to overthrow the rightful king of Tira-Nor. You planned the destruction of this city." A long pause. The prosecutor lifted his chin, as though finding a lost heirloom among sewage. "You deserve to die. However, His Majesty King SoSheth is inclined to mercy. In view of your past service to this city, lest any mouse question the benevolence of their

Sovereign Lord, the King of Tira-Nor has ordered that your life be spared."

A sigh ran through the crowd. Relief. Gratitude. Disappointment.

"Henceforth you are exiled from the city of Tira-Nor and His Majesty's realm. You have until sundown tomorrow to find refuge in the north meadows. If you are found within the Known Lands after that time, your life is forfeit." The prosecutor turned to challenge the crowd with his gaze. "From the mice of Tira-Nor you will receive neither comfort nor aid. Lieutenant!"

ThuBrik stepped forward, one eyebrow raised. "My Lawd?"

The prosecutor blinked. "No. Not you. *You*. Lieutenant KoVeek. You will lead the kingsguard in a show of loyalty to our king. What do we give a traitor?"

Lieutenant KoVeek, JaRed's friend, stared with eyes wide. At last he said, "The king's enemies are my enemies."

A thin sneer played across the prosecutor's lips. "That was not my question."

KoVeek hesitated. His gaze rose to the mice of the commons, the militia, the dozens of kingsguard warriors who busied themselves with studying the packed earthen floor. "Disdain," he said at last.

The prosecutor's sneer widened. "Show us."

KoVeek's face hardened. He approached in a wide circle and stopped at JaRed's back.

JaRed turned and looked up, realizing too late why KoVeek had moved behind him.

"Show us," the prosecutor said again.

KoVeek's jaw moved, as though he were chewing something. A dried berry, a piece of leather, a curling leaf. When he spat, nothing came out.

"Yes." The prosecutor gloated. "That is what we give a traitor. And who is next?" He looked to the Cadridians.

ThuBrik bowed, stepped forward to tower over JaRed, and smiled. He displayed no signs of difficulty gathering saliva.

One by one they marched past him. MeerQo. HarVik. LimJik. First the kingsguard, then the mice of the Commons.

They don't understand what's happening. What's about to happen. They don't know what evil hunts them.

Some were gleeful in their spite. Others, like KoVeek, spat air, illustrating their divided allegiance with a wet puff. Many looked away when their turn came. NewFal, who worked next to him on a scavenging crew. NeVin, the gruff black-hair who helped him bury his brothers, Merry and Berry, after the siege of GoRec. Oli, who chatted incessantly about the weather. JaRed pitied them, in spite of his own pain.

The line grew. Kirsten. UnDrew. Deq.

ONE

JaRed's head throbbed. His left cheek pounded with a great pressure, a lump of clay crammed inside his flesh. The swelling drew his mouth into an awkward shape.

He could not tell them what he knew, that theirs were the faces of his nightmare. It was their bodies he saw when he slept, scratching the white-linen fog with stiff limbs, eyes staring like soap bubbles into a black sky.

Luk. Raz. The warrior kits, baffled at the strangeness of the universe, that their hero, once the pride of the commons, could have come to this.

JaRed closed his eyes to shut out their shame, but they did not vanish. In his mind, they beamed at him outside the ReDemec family chambers. Their faces contorted in his memory. Luk's eyes popped, and his jaw hung wide enough for a yawn, but he was too tongue-tied to speak. Raz, his brother, stuck out his chin. "I'm you!" he said, "And Luk is GoRec! See my white?" He pointed to a lump of fur on his head, slicked back with saliva. He referred to the patch of white fur that dropped across JaRed's eyes, white being the mark of a true Seer.

"I'm gonna kill that rat," Luk said. "Easy. Just like you. See?" He rose on hind legs no bigger than twigs. "HAARRGGHH!" he said, and kicked out at his brother, who tripped over his own tail. Raz bounced up, red-faced, and JaRed laughed.

A touch on his arm. JaRed opened his eyes, dispelling the memory.

Raz bent over him, whispered, "You didn't do it, did you?"

Before JaRed could reply, someone pushed the kits along.

Afterward, the commoners melted away. KoVeek remained with half a dozen kingsguard warriors, his face concealed in the mouth of one of the eastern tunnels that opened into the Great Hall.

"And now," the prosecutor said, staring at JaRed over his long snout as the last of the onlookers disappeared, "Lieutenant Thu—" he glanced toward the Cadridian. A smile played across his mouth. "Lieutenant KoVeek will escort you to the Mud Gate. You just have time to reach the North Meadows—if you hurry."

2

Kreeg

General Kreeg stood in the black shadow of a tree and watched as two rat warriors padded through the underbrush of the Dark Forest. Their faces still bore the blood streaks of the Ur'Lugh, the elite guard of the dead rat master, GoRec.

Kreeg watched as they stumbled and plodded through the dry crackling husks of leaves littering the forest floor. GoRec's scum didn't know how to walk on Winter's beard.

GoRec. *May his soul rot forever.* Dead at the teeth of an undersized mouse with the speed of a humming-bird and an iron claw for a fist.

Kreeg's own followers were, much like him, scrappers, rats who lived in the abandoned quarry on the south side of the White River. GoRec's doomed army had consumed Kreeg's carefully saved horde of food in a matter of days, leaving nothing for the winter. When GoRec died, the remnants of his army dissolved into the surrounding woodlands, drifting into skull-crews as the temperature plummeted and the wind began to howl through their shrinking hides.

Kreeg spat.

He recognized one of the Ur'Lugh.

He flicked his tail. A twitch that would be noticed on the opposite side of the deer trail below him. *Get ready*, the twitch meant. And, *almost time.*

"Ho there, rats of GoRec," Kreeg said. "What brings scum like you skulking through the North Wood?"

The Ur'Lugh, huge brutes with the size and ferocity of elite fighters, nearly jumped out of their skins.

"Who goes?" the largest of the two asked. "Where're you hiding?"

Kreeg stepped forward, out of shadow and into the failing light of day. It promised to be a cold night.

"Ahh," said the smaller rat, a mass of gray hair. "That'd be Corporal Kreeg, judging by the stupid look. Or is it Sergeant Kreeg now?"

Kreeg feigned a smile and sauntered closer. "And you'd be Hash and Boomer, unless I'm mistaken. Which I never am. Last I saw, you two were running away from your master as though Wroth himself nipped at your heels."

"Shut up," spat Hash, the larger of the two.

Kreeg picked disinterestedly at one claw. "But then, you weren't alone. In fact, I didn't see any of GoRec's vaunted Girl-ugh fighting that day."

"I said shut up." Hash growled, stepping forward, and Boomer fell in behind him.

Good. They're used to getting their way, used to intimidation fighting for them. "The problem with the truth," he said, "is that it doesn't care who it eats."

"What do you mean?"

"I mean to ask you some questions, and to save time, I'll do the talking until I give you permission to answer."

The challenge was clear, formal, and direct. Perfect, according to rat tradition, which honors position—and therefore size, strength, and audacity—above all else. Any rat could assert the right of command at any time, so long as he was willing to die earning it.

Kreeg's bluntness brought a stupid, over-confident smile to Hash's face.

Kreeg flicked his tail—just so—a second time, a flick with meaning. *I do this alone. I need no rat to second me.*

From their hiding place in the brush behind the Ur'Lugh came the answering flick. Kreeg's warriors would not intervene. He was on his own.

For just a moment the insane fear came over him again, the fear that one day he would need a second, and all he had slaved to prove would come to nothing.

So you want to be Master Rat, do you?

Fear sent a long shiver down Kreeg's spine, shook itself in a furious twist of his tail, and was gone.

Hash crouched, snarled, sprang, his mouth open, his foreclaws bared.

An attack without strategy, without imagination. Hash lacked respect for his enemy.

Stupid.

General Kreeg sidestepped and dipped his right shoulder. He raked War Claw, the long knifelike claw on his right forepaw, upward into Hash's soft underbelly.

Hash screamed, doubled over, and turned halfway around. He seemed, for an instant, about to launch a furious counterattack, for his face contorted with rage and a muscle high on his neck began to twitch. But then his breath left him, and the color drained from his snout. "Ah … it—it burns!"

"Yes," Kreeg said. "That is War Claw. Not for nothing am I called General." He shifted his weight and raised up, turning his face to Boomer, who stood very still under a bony finger of a twig. "And you?"

But Hash wasn't finished speaking. From the ground behind him, he called up, "What did you do to me?" His voice was a gasp, a dry heave, a blister in the perfect stillness.

"I killed you," Kreeg said. He did not take his eyes

off Boomer, nor did he turn around. "But your body doesn't know it yet."

As if in answer, Hash gurgled a sound like that of a baby fighting off sleep.

Boomer's gaze shifted from Kreeg to Hash, and back to Kreeg.

"And you?" Kreeg said again.

Boomer swallowed. Pursed his lips. Looked down. "Master."

Kreeg sniffed. "I can't hear you, corporal."

Boomer cleared his throat. "Master! I am ... at your bidding."

"Ah. I see. Yes. That is more sensible. Except of course that I have no use for Ur'Lugh. No use for GoRec's dung. Especially I have no use for a coward."

Kreeg flicked his tail.

His warriors bounded from their hiding places, grinning idiotically. They formed a semi-circle behind Boomer and four of them latched onto the unfortunate rat's legs to restrain him.

"But—"

Kreeg's temper snapped. "Shut up!"

The forest hushed. Boomer cringed.

"Now." Kreeg slipped the black gleaming point of War Claw under Boomer's chin, let the point of it indent the flesh. "I have some questions that you are going to answer."

Afterward, Kreeg left Boomer's body hanging over

a low frost-covered branch and headed home in darkness. Boomer had told him everything.

There were forty Ur'Lugh left. They lived in an abandoned hunter's cabin north of the pond, and they were led by a rat named BlaKote. They were planning a raid on Tira-Nor, which suited Kreeg's purpose perfectly.

The sky cleared, revealing stars as cold and brilliant as icicles.

3

JaRed

JaRed limped toward the Mud Gate, followed by KoVeek. The Commons dozed around them. The air grew colder here where the tunnel rose and entered the Mud Gate complex. They stood close to the surface. Outside, winter draped the plains in a brittle shroud.

A silhouette stepped in front of him in the tunnel, one paw raised as though in benediction. He did not need the light of a glowstone to recognize the mouse. "Prince JoHanan." His voice sounded like a rasp scraping metal. He bowed stiffly.

The prince's gaze fell from JaRed's bruised face to the smears of blood clotting his chest. "I'm sorry, Ja-Red. Until tonight, I didn't know what my father was capable of. If I'd known he was planning this, I would have..."

You'd have done what?

Silence.

TaMir's prophecy came back in a wave, the old Seer's fat hands, the knees swollen in age. *You have been appointed by the Maker of Tails and Teeth, by the Bringer of Snow and Song, by the Source of Wind and Wisdom.*

Treason.

"It's over now," JaRed said.

"It isn't over," JoHanan whispered. "I learned an hour ago that my father still plans to kill you. You'll be ambushed at the border of the North Meadows."

JaRed worked the puzzle in his mind. King SoSheth meant to kill him far from Tira-Nor, someplace unseen. It made sense. To the south lay the White River, and to the west stood the houses of men. In the east, remnants of GoRec's army haunted the Dark Forest, Ur'Lugh rats with a taste for mouse flesh. SoSheth would expect him to seek food and friendship among the light-hearted outlanders of the North Meadows.

"Thank you for the warning," he said. "But I'm not going north yet."

JoHanan held up one paw. "Don't tell me where. I don't want to have to lie if he asks me where you went."

JaRed nodded. In truth, he knew only that he would head east and bide his time in the shadows of

the Dark Forest. He would watch and listen. A new
enemy threatened the city of Tira-Nor, an enemy that
lacked shape and definition. He felt it as clearly as he
felt the breath of winter sweeping down the long
throat of the tunnel.

"Tira-Nor is in danger," he said. "Your father is in
danger. And I don't know if he can save himself."

"Then I'll save him. You just look out for yourself."

"You've been a good friend."

JoHanan looked away, toward the guard chambers
at the sloping hole of the Mud Gate. "You'll be back.
Someday."

Someday, yes. JaRed turned and began the slow as-
cent to the gate hole. He thought of TaMir kneeling,
gathering one of JaRed's paws into his own, his voice
far away. *Someday they will all kneel as I do. Ja-
Red—Runt—you are the next king of Tira-Nor!*

Alone, JaRed limped across the moon-swept turf of
the open prairie to the edge of the Dark Forest. The
night air slipped through his fur with chilling fingers,
promising snow. A week or two, perhaps, and then
the bitter cold.

For a moment his confidence drained away. How
would he survive? Without food, without shelter? No
time to gather nuts and berries for the cold months
ahead. He would be forced to scavenge daily in an un-

familiar and forbidding realm.

In his mind he saw Luk and Raz again, eyes open, ribs poking through fur over distended bellies.

Tira-Nor cannot survive!

Too little food remained after GoRec's siege. Drought and war had withered the city's storerooms. Unless spring came early, many in the Commons would face starvation.

JaRed came to the edge of the Dark Forest and plunged in, turning south as the moon slid across the black seed-hole of ElShua's garden. The darkness of the forest welcomed him. His feet barely touched the dry leaves of autumn. He moved like a shadow among the fallen twigs and rotting nettles of the forest floor. He excelled at moving soundlessly, at making himself small and unnoticed, at disappearing.

He found the first body hanging across the lowest branch of a sapling, the blood at its throat steaming in the frosty night air.

A rat.

Its death-smell would draw predators. And yet a mystery lurked here. A clue, perhaps, to the nightmares that haunted him.

He searched the perimeter and found a second body rigid in death, its mouth locked open, the only wound a thin, almost bloodless slice along the belly.

JaRed nudged the stiffening arms and noticed the blood-streaks on its cheeks, the distinctive war-markings of Ur'Lugh.

GoRec's army. The Ur'Lugh almost destroyed Tira-Nor.

Revulsion rose in his throat. He hated the Ur'Lugh.

And yet, something about the dead rat's posture provoked a stab of pity. The eyes. The paws grasping for something, even in death. This brute's end was lonely and tortured. JaRed wished no such fate on anyone, even Ur'Lugh.

He heard the soft snick of a cracking leaf too late.

He turned to bolt, but a dozen rats surrounded him.

One of the rats smiled and flicked the long shining claw of his right paw in the air. "I don't believe we've met, mouse."

JaRed stumbled in the darkness, tripped by one of the rat guards who shoved him from behind. His face slammed forward and struck the frost-covered stump of a fallen tree.

The rats laughed and yanked him upright.

"WoKot?" General Kreeg's voice beat the air in a series of staccato explosions. "Why are we stopped?"

WoKot shrugged and looked back, his eyes as hard and narrow as nails. "Dunno. Listen up, vermin! I want hustle from here on, see? No more delays. And quit funnin' with the pris'ner."

"Aye, boss," JaRed's guard gave him a push. "'Ear

that, mate? Yer to quit playin' games, says the boss. 'Er I'll clout you one for good. Har har har."

The night dragged on, a nightmare sprint through bramble, thorn, and leafless underbrush. His guards chose a torturous path, shoving him into trees, rolling him in muck, kicking him when he fell.

Just before dawn they came to the White River. To the west, the Winding Cliffs dipped down, scowling over the river at barely the height of full grown elm. But here they arched upward like the curve of a great spine, and the foaming rush of the river at the cliff's base below blurred in the distance.

Draped in moonlight, a felled tree spanned the river from cliff to cliff. One of the tree fathers from the far side of the river, an oak of vast height and girth. Upended, its shattered roots jutted upward from its trunk like fingers. Its midsection sagged where it forked into innumerable limbs, but its branchy fingers gripped the cliff on the north side, defying the river in an arc that made JaRed think of a back breaking. Leaves, rusting to their winter stems, still clung tenaciously to their anchors.

JaRed's heart sank. *Perhaps ElShua is against us. The bridge must be the work of some great force of nature. And who rules the wind if not the one who sent it from His nostrils?*

The rats led him to the edge of the cliff. One of them clutched the fur of JaRed's neck in a silent show of power. "One push," the rat whispered in JaRed's ear. "And it'd be bye bye mousey." But his back straightened and his sneer melted as Kreeg approached.

"The sun is rising," Kreeg said, glancing in JaRed's direction. "We're on schedule. I hope our guest isn't afraid of heights."

This brought a few nervous laughs. The rats shifted uneasily, their fear evident. Clearly they didn't relish crossing the river.

WoKot peered over the side of the cliff. "All right, scum. Who's first?"

The rats cast hesitant glances at each other. One pointed to JaRed. "How 'bout him?"

Kreeg spat, sucking his teeth in the silence. After a long and very loud pause, he said, "We could do that, yes. That's an idea."

The rats smiled, nodded. From the back came a voice, "'Ow 'bout him,' I says, and what's the boss say? 'E says that's an idea."

Kreeg sniffed the icy air. "As I was saying, that is an idea. A stupid idea. Perhaps the worst idea I have heard all month. WoKot, what is that fool's name?"

WoKot leaned up on his back legs to get a glimpse of the fool who had spoken. "Tung."

"Tung. Yes. Well. Private Tung. Thou art well named, I see. Do you know why your idea is stupid?"

The other rats drew back, leaving Tung in a lonely

circle.

"Um…"

"No." Kreeg spat. "That is not the reason."

Snickering in the crowd.

"Think for a moment, Private Tung. If the mouse is sent over first, who will guard him? Who will stop him from running away?"

Understanding crept across Tung's face.

"No, Private Tung. The first to cross the river will in fact be you. You will go first, Private Tung. You will find a safe path across the bridge. You will find the frost patches. And if perhaps you slip and fall to your death, then you will at least die knowing that you did so for good reason, and not for some stupid plan you concocted yourself."

Tung shot a hateful glance at JaRed and licked his lips. "'Aye, boss." He grunted. "Glad to oblige."

"Good. Then lead on. I will be right behind you."

Tung hesitated a moment longer. Then he shuffled into the tangle of branches that marked the head of the tree. A moment later the others followed.

"That's it, then," JaRed's guard said. "Let's go."

In the crisp air of dawn JaRed's breath came in white cotton explosions. His legs shook with fatigue.

He hauled himself up the thickening branch to where it joined the main trunk of the tree and risked a glance over the side. Far below him, the swollen current lashed at the walls of the cliffs on either side. Its surface churned with broken limbs and unidentifiable debris.

"Wot's wrong, Mousey?" the rat guard asked. "Doesn't like water? Er is it heights yer 'fraid of?"

JaRed gripped the stump of a broken branch, grateful for the anchor. In truth, water terrified him.

He looked back at the supporting limbs sprouting from the bridge on the north side. In astonishment, he realized that the smaller limbs did not bear the weight of the tree. Rather, a limb on the underside of the trunk thrust at an angle into the cliff face, forming an arc that held the bridge aloft. If that weight-bearing branch were to lose its grip on the cliff face, the bridge would collapse.

A shriek split the air. A long trailing sound of utter terror. He wheeled and saw a lump of fur plunge into the river.

Far downstream, Tung's snout surfaced. Rat paws flailed the water.

The snout disappeared.

JaRed froze. The rat guards behind him stared into the distance.

From the far end of the bridge Kreeg's voice rang out, sad and clear as the sun leaped the horizon and kissed their faces. "Ah, poor Tung! A good rat. A good soldier. Alas, he never could keep his mouth shut."

JaRed's guard crept forward, leaned under a

branch, and peered into the chasm below.

JaRed turned and looked behind him, careful not to make a sound. He stood alone. His eyes found a patch of open ground between tangled branches.

He saw the path in his mind, the best—and perhaps last—opportunity he would have at life and freedom. Jump to the ground. Slide through leaf and bough to cliff's edge. Then sprint through shadow, cloaked by bush and tree. He would move north and east, deeper into the heart of the forest.

And how will I find out what Kreeg is plotting? When will I get a better opportunity to unmask Tira-Nor's enemy than I have now?

Resentment flooded through him. He closed his eyes against the force of it, tried to shove it away through sheer force of will.

If I stay, Kreeg will probably kill me. But if I don't...

KahEesha smiled. HaRed shrugged. KoVeek looked away. Luk and Raz said at the same time, *"You didn't do it, did you?"*

JaRed stood very still.

The moment slipped away.

His guard shuddered, turned, and looked into Ja-Red's face. Then his eyes shifted to the empty space behind him. A lump on his throat bobbed, and he said, "Move."

They navigated the bridge in silence. Frost made the surface slippery, and halfway across the branches ended, leaving nothing to grip.

At the far end JaRed heaved himself over the up-ended root system and lowered himself paw-by-paw to the ground with a sigh of relief.

"Safe and sound, are we?" Kreeg said.

"Don't know yet."

Kreeg smiled. "Indeed. What's your name, mouse?"

"JaRed. Son of ReDemec."

"From Tira-Nor?"

"I'm not welcome in Tira-Nor."

Kreeg gazed at him without expression. "A point in your favor then."

They marched through a wide-open glade, the earth quilted in patches of orange sunlight and split by the long shadows of trees. Kreeg and the rats seemed to relax.

A building loomed before them, squatting on a concrete-block foundation. Paint peeled from it in thick flakes. The door, secured by a rusting chain, sagged behind a spray of dead grass rising through the threshold. Dirt-blackened windows glared like empty sockets from a skull.

They approached from the east, over a gravel drive long since given way to brown-bladed weeds. They entered through a hole in a basement window.

The place reeked of hunger. Disease and starvation hung in the air like smoke.

Rats huddled everywhere. Females and young rats.

Ancient rats whose teeth rotted and whose fur hung in clumps. Sick rats. Starving rats. Dying rats.

"What do we do with him?" WoKot asked.

"Put him in the hole," Kreeg said.

JaRed was led to a corner of the basement, a hole in the foundation wall, and shoved in. He fell in darkness, landed on stone.

"Nighty night, Mousey," a voice said. "If you get hungry, just knock. Maybe we'll throw down something from home later on. Har har har."

Something from home? What did that mean?

A stone groaned in front of the hole, and JaRed found himself in utter blackness.

4

HaRed

Someone stroked HaRed's forehead. His skull felt like a summer melon about to burst. He tried to move, but a voice cooed at him.

"Hold still."

He remembered. Cadridians. JaRed's beating. A blow to the back of his head.

KahEesha knelt over him. "Hold still."

He licked his lips. "Did they hurt you?"

She shook her head.

"Where's JaRed?"

"Father is trying to find out."

HaRed rose, the world swaying around him like a hammock from which he could not escape. Light from a glowstone stabbed his eyes. He thrust up an arm to deflect it, and collapsed.

"I told you," KahEesha said.

"We have to help him."

"Of course."

"The king wants him dead."

"You can't go anywhere in your condition, brother."

HaRed glared at her, nausea roiling in his stomach. "You're the pregnant one, sister."

Father appeared in the chamber entry, his expression grave. "JaRed is alive."

"Alive." KahEesha sighed.

Father shuffled into the chamber and settled next to HaRed. "But SoSheth sent him into exile, and there are rumors of an ambush near the border of the North Meadows."

HaRed tried to rise, his stomach twisting in protest. "I'll go to him. Warn him. The king—"

KahEesha touched the lump on the back of HaRed's head with delicate fingers, as though checking an egg for cracks. "Not until the swelling goes down."

Father shook his head. "No, son. The king has forbidden anyone speaking to him. SoSheth will have you both killed."

"But—"

Father held up one paw for silence. "JaRed was trained in the kingsguard. He can move silently. He's better off on his own."

HaRed grimaced. "Thanks."

FOUR

"I mean it, son."

"I will talk to my husband when he returns," KahEesha said. Blang, captain of the kingsguard, remained one of JaRed's most loyal friends.

Father nodded. "Yes. But now we know why the king sent him away."

"What about TaMir?" KahEesha asked.

"He hasn't much influence in the palace these days. I think going to him would only make matters worse."

HaRed bit his lower lip. "This is my fault."

"Nonsense," Father said. "I'll hear no more about it. Captain Blang—"

"But, Father—"

"No! I've lost your mother and four sons. I will not lose you. I forbid it." Father's chin quivered. He sighed heavily. "I forbid it," he said again, and stumped out of the chamber.

HaRed swallowed the familiar lump in his throat. "Father must deal with his grief in his own way. I must try to help JaRed."

"Yes."

"This is all my fault."

"Ha! You are not that important, brother."

"I betrayed him, KahEesha. I told SoSheth about TaMir's prophecy."

He expected this to surprise her, but she said, very quietly, "I know. TaMir told me."

HaRed's nausea grew. A sick feeling of despair and

shame. "TaMir knew?"

"He is a Seer. What did you expect?"

"I don't know. I guess I didn't ... believe."

"And now you do?"

"Now?" HaRed stared at the ceiling. "I still don't know. I don't know anything, really."

KahEesha laughed. "You are so predictable, HaRed, son of ReDemec." She leaned close and whispered in his ear. "But you have changed. Even TaMir says so."

"TaMir again? Did he say anything else?"

Her eyes sparkled. "Yes."

5
Blang

Captain Blang arrived late at the palace hall. A feeling of doom gnawed at his gut, as tenacious as a dog worrying a bone.

King SoSheth paced the dais at the far end, glaring at the courtiers arrayed before him. "You." SoSheth jabbed his finger for emphasis. "You there. Yes, you. What is your name?"

The mouse blinked, one paw held over his chest. He spoke with the breathy accent of a Cadridian. "Me, majesty?"

"You."

"I am called YaGo, highness." The mouse gave a sweeping bow. "Your humble servant."

"YaGo? I have never heard of you, YaGo."

"I am from Cadrid. My father, the king—"

SoSheth held up one paw. "Yes yes. But where

have you been? And who asked you to be here? And why were you so late? Don't you know what it means to be summoned to an emergency meeting in the palace? If it weren't for the many years of friendship between myself and your father, whose name escapes me at the moment, I would have you punished."

YaGo bowed again, a soundless apology. His head swooped forward in a long arc, the current fashion in the court at Cadrid, but his eyes remained fixed on the king's hind feet.

"Where is Captain Blang? And where is Prince Jo-Hanan? Where is my son?" SoSheth stopped pacing and glared at the royal prosecutor.

"I don't know, Majesty."

"You would think," SoSheth said, "that even a great fool like my son could find time to protect his inheritance."

Captain Blang cleared his throat. "Majesty. I am here."

"Ah. So good of you to come, captain. I pray you didn't overexert yourself in getting here so quickly."

Blang glanced at the faces of the other counselors. Nothing he could say would change the king's mood. He decided to keep his mouth closed.

Standing in the center of the earthen platform, King SoSheth motioned to the prosecutor. "Tell them."

The prosecutor bowed and turned to the rest of the

mice. He was, perhaps, the only friendless mouse in all of Tira-Nor. A faint sneer played across his lips. "As some of you are doubtless aware, we have uncovered a plot against the king."

Heads whipped around. Whispers cut the silence of the room.

"I call you as witnesses," SoSheth said. "So that none may hereafter accuse me of injustice. Captain Blang?"

"Yes, my lord?" Standing in the back of the room, Blang hesitated. He stood in a glass cage, unable to free himself.

SoSheth spoke through clenched teeth. "You will escort us now to the chamber of TaMir the Seer. We shall hear the truth of this thing for ourselves."

Blang led them through the palace and kingsguard sections of the city. A train of professional gossips, nabobs, and yea-sayers twittered in his wake.

He paused in the tunnel connecting the Kingsguard to the Commons. *TaMir? Treason?* The knot in his stomach twisted into coiled-snake. *The king is mad!*

He entertained the idea that the king would tire of this game and end it. Blang had seen SoSheth in tirades before, seen fits of madness and outbursts of rage dissolve like clouds before the wind. Tears of rage turned to a humorless laugh. "You fools!" the king would say. "Ha! Don't you know when your king jests?"

SoSheth stalked past him. The king led them east, down, then east again. Deeper in. Farther from the palace. To the hovels of the poor.

They paused for the king to remove a glowstone from its place high in the wall. No one had thought to bring light, for none of them—save Blang—ever ventured so far into the Commons, and none knew how dark its tunnels could be. Few glowstones found their way into the tunnels of the ordinary citizens of the city.

The group rounded a last turn and the king hesitated for the first time. An expression of doubt crossed his face. A look of regret, followed by resolve. The moment didn't last.

The king entered the chamber without even scratching at the mud frame to announce his presence. The others followed, but Blang waited in the tunnel until the sound of the king's voice reminded him of his sworn duty. Grimly, he stepped into the chamber of the Seer, TaMir.

They stood in a semi-circle around the old mouse, their faces ominous in the blue-green light of the stone.

TaMir faced them, his back straight. On the walls of his chamber, weird pictures were etched into the time-hardened mud. "My lord," he said. His gaze shifted to the radiating glowstone. "It is long since you last graced my home with your light."

"Where is JaRed?"

"Exiled. Or so I am told."

"He has disappeared."

TaMir raised one eyebrow. "Wasn't that your intention?"

"Don't waste my time, you old fool!"

Blang shoved two nincompoop sons-of-somebody out of his way and stood behind the king.

"Time?" TaMir said softly. "Time? You have precious little left, my lord."

The king's jaw dropped.

"Did you think you could rob ElShua of His words? Come back to your senses, King! Give Tira-Nor back to ElShua while the choice is still yours!"

"Where did JaRed go?" So faint, the words. Like lightning cracking at a great distance.

TaMir shrugged. "He fled Tira-Nor to become its king."

SoSheth growled. "For that, you will die."

Blang stepped forward, out of the circle of busy-bodies and do-nothings. Never had he challenged the storm of SoSheth's temper. "My lord and king, do not do this."

King SoSheth wheeled and struck him across one cheek with open claws. Blang felt the sting of it, the slices turning to streaks of blood that dribbled down his face.

"You!" SoSheth said. "Get out. Get out! GET OUT!"

Blang did not move, though every impulse of habit screamed at him to obey, to get out, to not risk open refusal. Had he not sworn to obey this king he had once loved? Had he not vowed his allegiance? He looked up into the king's eyes, saw only deep emptiness.

"My lord," he said. Grasping for something. Anything. Life and hope slipped away from him, falling, dripping like the blood that flowed from his face and spattered the dirt floor.

The king struck him again, his paw clenched into a fist that slammed into Blang's nose and hurled him backward.

Pain erupted behind Blang's eyes, but after a moment he managed to pull himself to all fours and stand, swaying. "My lord," he said again. "TaMir is the only Seer in the city. What will you do when the voice of ElShua is gone?"

The King advanced and struck him a third time, and this blow carried more force, more of his weight. It landed on Blang's opposite cheek. His claws ripped through Blang's fur, drew four long gashes on his lower jaw. "I will celebrate," SoSheth said. He turned to the other mice. "Who will kill this fat old fool for me?" He glanced from face to face.

Silence.

From the floor, Blang said, "I beg you, do not do it!" And now his voice shook, for he could not stand, could not leave, could not turn away.

SoSheth kicked him in the ribs once, twice, a third time. "Is there no one willing to carry out the desire of the king? No one who wishes to take Blang's place as Captain of the Kingsguard?"

From the shadows a voice answered. "The desire ahv the King is my desire. His will is my will." The Cadridian, YaGo, stepped forward and waited above Captain Blang's heaving body.

"My time has come," TaMir said to YaGo. "But even Kalla will not save you in the end."

For just a moment, surprise fluttered across YaGo's face.

TaMir lowered himself to his swollen knees. His eyes found Blang's, and he forced a smile. One last fruit falling from a dying tree. "Thank you, my friend."

6

JaRed

JaRed turned on the cold slab of rock and stared up into the gaping darkness.

Sounds echoed in the black emptiness of the hole: the far-off patter of rats, the occasional scratching of who-knew-what, and, from somewhere high overhead, the wet sound of moisture splat-splat-splatting against rock.

A bodiless whisper hissed at him in the silence. He was stupid not to run when he had the chance. The rats had buried him alive. He would starve to death. He would die of thirst. He would suffocate. There was no escape.

ElShua had abandoned him.

Sealed by a flat stone, the entry hole loomed tantalizingly close. A pale blade of indirect sunlight, thinned to the color of dirty water, seeped through the crack between the rock and the cinder-block wall. The crack might be wide enough to slip through, but he could not reach it.

"Quit shoving me," a female voice said from above.

A rat answered. "Move faster, then."

The rock groaned sideways. Figures stood silhouetted against a smear of yellow light. JaRed blinked and held one arm across his face.

"I can't see," the female said.

"Don't need to see. Only way to go is down. Har har har." The rat guard gave her a shove.

She teetered, arms pinwheeling, and fell.

"Har har har," the rat called down. "Keep quiet now or there'll be nothin' thrown down later."

Nothing thrown down. No food, was what he meant. No flaking chunks of dried soap to tease the belly.

"Are you all right?" JaRed asked.

She gasped. "Who are you? Where are you? Well? Say something!"

"I'm here in the corner. No need to shout. No one else can hear you."

"Who are you?"

"JaRed. Son of ReDemec the Red."

"From Tira-Nor?"

"Yes. JaRed of Tira-Nor."

"Oh."

Water splatted in the distance.

"You killed GoRec."

JaRed held out his paws in the darkness. He could not see them. The suffocating blackness of the room reminded him of GoRec's eyes.

GoRec. Were these the paws?

"Yes," he said. "I killed GoRec."

"Is it true what they say about you? That TaMir made you king over Tira-Nor?"

JaRed closed his eyes, took in the smell of her. She hailed from one of the families. "He didn't make me king. He just ... He said that someday ..."

JaRed sighed.

TaMir's prophecy had brought him only misery.

<hr/>

The old seer's lips quivered. "Just a moment." His balding tail twitched, and his eyes rolled up into his head as though searching for distant memory. "Ah! Yes. Now I have it." He smiled. "What is it, JaRed?"

"Why?" JaRed asked again. "Why did you choose me?"

TaMir's brow sank into a dark scowl. "I didn't choose you. Don't you recall? I said so very clearly. The problem with young people is that they don't listen."

"But—"

"I told you. ElShua picked you, not me. If it were up to me ... well. No, that isn't what I meant to say."

His scowl softened. His shoulders slumped, and he let out a long sigh. He pointed to one corner of his chamber. "What is that?"

In the darkness, JaRed could see nothing but a black shadow. TaMir's glowstone lit the chamber poorly. The weird etchings of his walls were indistinguishable. JaRed retrieved a brown nut seed from the corner and held it up. "This?"

"Yes. What is it?"

"An acorn."

"Ah," TaMir said. "Yes. Even so." He took the acorn from JaRed and set it on the dirt between them. "That is why I anointed you. And it is why you are not yet a Seer. You see an acorn, and I see an oak tree."

———

What if TaMir is wrong? What if I'm not made king? Would it mean ElShua can't be trusted?

Or would it mean ElShua doesn't exist at all?

JaRed swallowed, his mouth dry. "TaMir just said that I would be king some day. But he didn't say when or how." The words echoed in the dark. The soundless black whisper came again, mocking him. *Your hope is a lie!*

The female answered his explanation with silence.

"We must find out what Kreeg is up to," JaRed said. "After that, you'll have to get word back to Tira-

Nor."

"Kreeg?"

"The rat leader."

"You know him?"

"No. Just his name."

"What do you intend to do?"

"Escape. Find out as much as we can about these rats and get the information back to Captain Blang. He needs to know about all of this. The rats, the bridge, the quarry."

More cold silence. Had he offended her? Said something uncouth or presumptuous? He went over the conversation in his mind and realized he had overlooked common courtesy.

"Forgive me," he said. "I haven't asked you your name."

"DeStra WilloWind."

"Ah. Yes. I've heard of you."

"Whatever do you mean?"

"I don't mean anything. Just that I've heard of you."

"Why shouldn't you have heard of me?"

"Tira-Nor is a big city. You're from one of the Greater Families. I'm from the Commons. Not much mixing between them."

"My father is an important mouse. The whole city knows who he is."

"Your father. Yes."

"What do you have against the Families, anyway?" She sounded angry now. "Who are you to be king? You're a Commoner! Besides, even the Commons doesn't claim you now. The whole city knows you're a traitor."

She turned her back to him in the darkness, as though to say, this conversation is over.

JaRed lay in silence, remembering Tira-Nor's short-lived gratitude after his killing of GoRec. The smiles of his friends. The elaborate bows. The applause as his name was cheered at the autumn feast.

He lay very still and listened.

Splat-splat-splat.

7

Kreeg

G eneral Kreeg entered the unwelcome stink of
the quarry basement with a sense of dread. He
hated this place. After the clean air of the night, the
stench of it assaulted his nostrils. Bitterness welled up
in his gut like bile. Sickness and death enshrouded the
building.

We won't last through the winter.

WoKot sniffed. "Um." He shifted from one muscular leg to the other. "And, um, then again..."

Kreeg ignored him, took two steps into the warm
morning light piercing the grimy windows. Dust
swirled, dancing before him as he stumped to the floor
of the cellar.

The eyes of the poordevils followed him, unblinking.

WoKot bounded down after him. "Er, boss—"

Kreeg zigzagged through the poordevils. These sick ones, strewn like garbage across the dirty floor. These dying bodies with the life seeping from them in puddles. These starving youngsters with eyes that stared through everything and into the ultimate black emptiness at the center of the universe.

Oddly, a few of them still hoped.

Stupid. They were going to die. Kreeg could not stop it. Would not stop it even if he could.

And yet they gazed at him when he walked among them, staring as though he carried miracles in his fingertips.

Hope? No. Hope is a lie.

Nature had made its choice. These will live. And these will die. Facts as irresistible as the White River under flood.

WoKot drew near again. "Um, boss?"

"Shut up," Kreeg said.

"Right." WoKot sniffed. The sniff said, "Okay, but don't blame me!" The sniff said, "You're going to be angry later." It said, "I know how to take orders, even when they're stupid."

The sniff irritated Kreeg. He sighed. "Did you put that other mouse in the hole?"

"Yes."

"All right. What is it?"

"News. From Tira-Nor."

Kreeg's ears swiveled.

"One of my lookouts came in after Huchek's patrol. Skulker. A reliable rat. Says a kingsguard mouse approached him under a sign of truce. Says mousey wants to meet with General Kreeg. Says he has information."

Kreeg scowled. "What does he want?"

"Don't know. But mousey gave a pledge. Said four patrols would leave the city within twenty minutes, looking for someone."

"Looking for who?"

"Don't know that, either. But it happened, boss. Four squads of fighters. Twenty four mice. Then he said if you wanted more, to meet him in the spot you did those two Ur'Lugh at midnight tomorrow. I thought you'd want to know the up-and-up."

Kreeg raised one eyebrow. "Four squads? The mouse king is in earnest. He wants someone badly. How many rat fighters can we muster in a pinch?"

WoKot shrugged. "Depends on whether any more go down with the fever. At best, maybe sixty."

Kreeg wheeled and trotted past the rats on the floor, leapt up the steps, and padded through the open doorway. His private quarters lay at the end of a hallway behind a locked door. He squeezed through the gap under the door and paced the oil-stained carpet. WoKot squeezed through behind him.

"Looking for someone," Kreeg said to himself.

"Yes."

"What else did Skulker tell you?"

"Nothin' else. Said he saw four squads o' mice come up outta the ground like it couldn't stand the taste of 'em and it was spewin' em back out. Said they was in a awful hurry."

Kreeg cursed. He was tired, though he didn't let that show. He wanted nothing more than to rest and sharpen his hatred in silence. And yet, here grew an opportunity.

"Um."

Kreeg inhaled. His eyes narrowed. "Um, what?"

"Well. I was thinking. Maybe you should ask that little runt. Maybe he knows who the king of Tira-Nor is hunting."

Kreeg's gaze shifted to the window, then back to WoKot. "Yes." A thought began to assemble in his brain.

"Yes?"

"Shut up!" Kreeg snarled.

WoKot's lower jaw snapped shut in a kind of salute, and he waited in silence with pinched eyes.

Power rose in Kreeg's limbs. It welled up in his legs, coursed through his spine, shoulders, and neck. A wave of strength and emotion wrapped warmth around him like a winter coat. Tired as he was, he knew what he must do.

He knew who the mouse was, the little "runt" languishing in the dungeon below him. Strange fate! Ha!

He felt he could conquer the world!

The runt would be Tira-Nor's undoing, would help him tear down the mouse city without even realizing it.

"I know now, WoKot. I know how to destroy Tira-Nor!" Kreeg wheeled on WoKot and his voice rang like a church bell in the frigid morning air. "Bring him to me, WoKot! Bring both prisoners to me! Well? What are you waiting for? Bring me the runt!"

WoKot turned and fled.

When he stood alone in the room, Kreeg strode to the corner and leapt into the seat of a chair that stood behind a dust-caked desk. Its cushion leaked white stuffing from a split longer than Kreeg's body, but from it he could look down into the black mouth of the desk drawer.

He nudged open the drawer and slipped inside, where a more deadly smell greeted him; a smell that overpowered the stench of the basement.

In the back of the drawer he found the jar, still more than half-full of dark liquid. He pried back the lid, slid the covering to one side, and held his breath as he reached into the jar with his right forepaw.

Afterward, he screwed the lid back on, shoved the drawer closed, and slipped under the door into the hallway.

8

JaRed

A scream ripped through the foul black air of the dungeon. It echoed off the cold rock walls and mixed with the splat-splat-splat of moisture dripping from above.

JaRed shivered.

In his dream he stood alone in the Dark Forest. Fog swirled around him in a cold sheet. Here and there the black skeletons of trees stabbed the mist, pinned to a tapestry the color of dull steel. He could not see the sun, though wisps of light melted into the shadows of the trees in colorless pools.

He called for a sentry, expecting soldiers from the kingsguard, but no one answered.

Silence hung thick and heavy in the air. Nothing moved. The fog itself seemed motionless, as though it had inhabited that place forever, and would remain long after JaRed was gone.

He called again.

Nothing. No movement anywhere.

He moved toward the looming shadow of an elm. Snow dusted the matted grass and curling leaves of the forest floor. JaRed's breath came in puffs of white that were lost against the vast curtain surrounding him.

He saw the body suddenly, blood coming from a gash in its throat and congealing in a shallow earthen dimple scratched into the frost-hardened ground.

He did not want to look, did not want to see whose face the body belonged to. But he could not turn away. Not now.

He stepped forward, as though pushed by some invisible hand. The fog clung to him like paste; every breath hung heavily in his chest.

The air thrummed, a sound like the beating of a million wings, and starlight pierced the dense fog in shafts of white fire.

Then the insane scream came again. High and terrified and furious. It rebounded through the dungeon and exploded into JaRed's nightmare, rolling through the shadows like the sound of Wroth's laughter in the old legends. *You'll regret this!*

"Are you all right?" DeStra asked.

JaRed opened his eyes. "What?"

Silence. Then, her voice a whisper, "I'm hungry."

Hungry.

The faces of his dream returned in a rush, skin drawn tight against bone. The voice of his rat guard. *"Maybe we'll throw down something from home later on. Har har har."*

All at once he understood what would happen. He blinked, straining to see DeStra's face in the darkness. "Kreeg's planning a raid on Tira-Nor."

"He doesn't have enough rats for that. Does he?"

"He'll go in through the Wind Gate. Or East Gate. He's desperate. All he needs is access to the store-rooms."

"But ... But ... I don't believe it. That's impossible. The kingsguard will stop him."

"Maybe."

"What are we going to do?"

JaRed clenched his teeth. Perhaps he owed Tira-Nor nothing. The mice of the Commons had rejected him. Despised him. Spit on him. And yet, he couldn't abandon them.

He stood and stretched, thin with his own hunger. "We're going to escape."

"What ... How?"

He groped his way to the wall beneath the entry hole. Earlier, he thought if he could find something to stand on, he might be able to force his way through the crack between the rock and the wall.

She stumbled toward him, her paws groping. "What are you doing?"

"Do you mind kneeling?"

"Why?"

"So I can climb onto your shoulders."

"I will not!"

"All right." He sighed. "Forget it. We'll just stay here and rot. We can listen to the nice dripping sounds. Smell the fungus. Taste the soap chips."

A pause. "If you ever tell anyone about this, I'll kill you." DeStra knelt. "You're a commoner!"

JaRed hoisted himself to her shoulders. "Really? But there were dozens of people I wanted to tell."

He could just reach the gap with his outstretched fingers. He slid the palm of his left forepaw into the crack. The stone felt cool to the touch. "Trapped in Kreeg's dungeon! With DeStra WilloWind. What a laugh!" He tested his grip with short tugs against the rock. "Pitch darkness. Horrible foul odors. And nasty sounds day and night. And then, to get out I used her for a ladder. Oh, yes, that's one for the kingsguard."

"You're repulsive. Ow!"

The soft object on which he stubbed his toe was apparently her ear. "Yes, you told me that yesterday." He sprang upward, heaving with all his might and kicking against the chalky wet surface of the wall.

For a moment he thought he wouldn't make it. He hung suspended in nothingness for a long time, his legs kicking for traction. But then his right leg caught a toe-hold and his knee slammed into the ledge against the inner surface of the stone barricade.

He pressed his arm into the crack. The stone did not lay flush against the cinder-block wall, but leaned against it at an angle, the crack widening near the floor. By heaving with all his might, he could move the stone a little and widen the crack higher up.

"Listen," he whispered. "I can't force the stone from this side, but I think I can fit through the crack. "Can you reach my tail?" He felt a sharp tug. "Okay. Pull yourself up. I'll help you. The extra weight ... Ow!"

Her weight hurt.

He couldn't move the stone by himself. But the extra weight of her body, leveraged properly, just might. He leaned against the rock, his teeth grinding, his eyes shut. His tail burned. The bones in his spine popped.

For a moment the stone didn't move. Then, slowly, it rolled sideways. A half inch. An inch. More.

Still holding onto the outer edge of the rock with one arm, he reached down with the other and pulled on his own tail, drawing DeStra up.

She scrabbled for a foothold, and seconds later they stood on the other side of the stone, blinking against the murky gray light of dawn filtering down from the casement window above them. Dust blanketed the floor. In the corner near an ancient water heater, a warped two-by-four ramped upward against the wall.

Its shadow ran into a black smear of mildew that stained the concrete blocks of the foundation.

DeStra turned her face to him. Young, attractive, defiant. Short-haired, with deep brown eyes.

Longing gripped him, unexpected in its intensity. Maybe someday, when all this was over ...

Then her eyes narrowed, and the thought died.

She stared at him, blinking as her eyes adjusted to the light. Her head turned to one side. Her mouth fell open. She wore a look of revulsion, as though he were leprous.

Why? What have I done?

She glanced away. Through clenched teeth she asked, "What now?"

JaRed pressed a finger to his lips. Sick and dying rats lay at the other end of the basement behind a dividing wall. From a doorless opening came the faint groans and snores of dozens of poordevils. He motioned for DeStra to help him roll the stone back into place over the hole.

"Leave it," she said. "Let's get out of here."

"Not yet," JaRed whispered.

He led her up the two-by-four ramp to the top of the concrete block wall. They stopped under a cool draft of air that whisked through a crack in the floor above them, carrying voices.

"Looking for someone," Kreeg said, his voice faint.

"Yes."

"What else did Skulker tell you?"

WoKot's reply was muffled, but a moment later, he said, more clearly, "Maybe you should ask that little runt. Maybe he knows who the king of Tira-Nor is hunting."

"Yes."

"Yes?"

"Shut up!"

Another pause, then Kreeg said, jubilant, "I know now, WoKot. I know how to destroy Tira-Nor! Bring him to me, WoKot! Bring both prisoners to me! I want them here in front of me in ten minutes! Well? What are you waiting for? Bring me the runt!"

JaRed stared at DeStra, whose face went pale. "They're coming for us."

"We should have gone out through the basement window."

"Too many rats beneath it."

"They're all sleeping."

"Haven't you been listening? Kreeg is planning to raid Tira-Nor's storerooms. He knows something we don't. When you get back to Tira-Nor, you must tell Captain Blang about Kreeg. About the bridge."

"If we get caught again it will be your fault."

"Get down!" JaRed shoved her shoulders into the cement top of the wall just as a rat lumbered through the doorway below. From above came a thud, then footsteps plodding away. Kreeg was leaving.

"Mousies!"

JaRed edged over and watched as the rat plodded to the corner of the basement and poked his snout into the crack between stone and hole.

"Eh, mousies? You still alive down there? 'Aven't keeled over, eh? Heh heh heh."

JaRed raised himself up on his hind legs and stuck his nose through the crack. Too small for a rat, the crack spread wide enough for him to squeeze through. He hesitated. He didn't want to go into Kreeg's war room, but they had to go somewhere, and they couldn't very well walk out the main exit.

He pointed to the crack in the floor above him. DeStra nodded. A moment later they slipped into the room and stood in a dim wash of murky light.

In the distance, a rat's voice assailed the gloom. "Mousies! Mooousies! Come on up, now!"

JaRed cast his gaze around the room. Before them, a desk squatted over a torn leather chair. Its drawers stood open, a beggar turning out empty pockets. Sunlight slanted through a grimy window over the desk, and against the far wall stood a file cabinet and an empty bookcase.

"Mousies? Mousies!"

He climbed the drawers as though they were steps and crossed the dusty blotter to the window. It was shut fast, with no gap between sash and sill.

"Someone's coming!" DeStra said.

68

Footsteps in the hall outside the door.

"MOUSIES!"

Sounds of confusion. An alarm. Raised voices. In moments, the basement would be crawling with ruffians roused by WoKot to begin the search. They could not go back through the crack. They would have to get out some other way.

"Come up here!" JaRed said. "Quickly!"

DeStra obeyed. She sprang up the drawers to the desktop and looked around. "Where are we going?"

"In there." JaRed pointed to the top drawer, then dropped into the opening without waiting to see if she would follow.

She thumped into the drawer next to him and huddled in the corner. "I told you we should have left!"

"Shhh!"

They waited.

Someone stood in the office behind the desk. Several someones, by the sound of their paws on the floor.

"WoKot." Kreeg's voice came from the chair. "You're an idiot. They're in here."

Kreeg's nose slid into the drawer under venomous eyes. He regarded them for a long while. "Interesting," he said at last. "Stupid. But interesting."

General Kreeg slumped against the cinder block wall. His gaze shifted between JaRed and DeStra, his eyes bloodshot. "Who are you?"

"I told you. My name is JaRed, son of ReDemec the Red."

"Of Tira-Nor?"

"I've been exiled."

"Ah," Kreeg said. "And what happened to you?"

"Happened?" JaRed glanced from Kreeg to DeStra, but she would not look at him.

Kreeg turned to WoKot. "How long has he been in the hole?"

"Five days and, uh ... two nights, boss. It was him we thinks, you know? That sound?" WoKot tapped his skull with one finger. "Small body, small brain, as mum al'ays used to say. Gone crazy, boss. He's the one, and no doubt."

Kreeg stared at JaRed a moment longer. "Odd." He turned to DeStra. "And you? Another fugitive?"

Her back straightened. "Of course not. Tira-Nor is my home. A fact I am quite proud of."

Kreeg smiled. "No doubt. And do you know this little mouseling here?"

"No," DeStra said. "He's an outlaw. He might as well be a rat."

Kreeg stared at her for just a moment, then he threw back his head and laughed. "Very well," he said, his eyes staring at the stained ceiling high overhead. From the basement came the rattling gasps of wounded and dying rats. "I cannot afford to feed you, and there has been enough killing for now. I am going to release both of you." A smile shadowed his face, as though at some private joke. "Whoever you are, your madness torments you better than WoKot ever could."

9
HaRed

"**B**igums! Got a newling here. Hails from Nor."

HaRed waited under the vast roof of RuHoff's cave. He blinked, his eyes struggling to adjust to the dim light fanning upward from the low opening.

"Nor? What's he want?"

HaRed's escort, an outlander with graying whiskers, nudged his elbow. "Dunno. But he says he's Ratbane's brother!"

Shapes moved in the gloom, took the form of mice as the room lost its darkness.

One very fat form in the back of the cave did not move. "Ratbane? A brother?"

"Says he."

"Ha!" The fat one chuckled. "That's good, Scrounger!"

In all, twenty three outlanders gathered in

NINE

RuHoff's cave. HaRed expected more.

Scrounger nudged his elbow again. "Go on, then. Tell Bigums what you told me."

HaRed glanced from face to face. The outlanders were not moving now. They seemed friendly, but HaRed didn't trust them.

He stepped forward, wondering how to address the outlander chief. Sire? Lord? King? No glowstones lit the chamber, and he couldn't read the fat mouse's face. He would have to guess.

He stopped exactly nine paces away and bowed. "Your Majesty." He licked his lips. Opened his mouth. Started to speak.

The room exploded with laughter. Bigums grabbed his enormous belly and rolled onto his back, his face contorted in the shadows, his shoulders shaking.

The outlanders lounging at the edges of the cave pointed, laughing with almost as much enthusiasm as their leader. Scrounger fell to his knees.

HaRed waited for the moment to pass. But just as the laughter degenerated into a quieter wave of snorts and giggles, someone to HaRed's left said, "Majesty," and the room erupted again.

Scrounger rose and grabbed the fur at the back of HaRed's neck. He said, "You'll address him as 'your worship' or not at all."

Bigums, struggling to rise, keeled over onto his

side, his chest heaving. He looked as though he were going to burst. His lips mouthed the words "My worship," and one hand flapped the air for quiet.

HaRed's eyes adjusted to the light. The legendary etchings of Glyn the Strong revealed themselves on the cave walls. Weird pictures that told stories from the past, present, and future. Plain as sunlight, and yet unfathomable.

After several more failed attempts at quiet—and several more interruptions—Bigums managed to re-seat himself, his back propped against the cave wall. "After that," he said at last, "I don't care what you came for. You can have it." He paused and looked around. "Up to half my kingdom."

There came a brief pause, then another round of laughter. Several mice stood and applauded.

"That's why he's the Bigums," someone said. "Downright generous, he is."

HaRed felt he couldn't take any more of this. He clenched his teeth, licked his lips, and took a step forward. Had he done that in the royal palace at Tira-Nor, an officer of the kingsguard would have shoved him back immediately. But the outlanders didn't notice. "I want to know if JaRed Ratbane made it here safely," he said.

The smiles faded. The room stilled.

Bigums leaned forward, his face split by a wide grin. "Lost him, have you?"

HaRed replied before anyone could make a wise-crack. "He's been exiled by King SoSheth."

Bigums pointed to his left at a place along the wall. "Maybe that's him there."

Water dribbled down the cave wall and disappeared into a crack in the stony, uneven floor. Streaks of red, outlined by a white scar on the rock surface, divided more of Glyn's etchings. Near the crack, a mouse skull grinned up at him.

"Not likely," HaRed said.

"Ratbane's coming here?" Scrounger asked.

"SoSheth set an ambush to kill JaRed at the border."

"I was wrong about you." Bigums sighed. "You've no sense of humor at all. Go away."

"Is it that hard to give straight answers?"

"Is it that hard," a voice mimicked, "to give straight answers?"

HaRed wheeled. A mouse stood there, frowning expansively, hands on his hips, a perfect imitation of HaRed's posture.

The outlanders roared. "That's him," someone hollered. "Him to the whisker."

Cold rage settled on HaRed's shoulders. He turned back to Bigums and stepped forward again, and then again.

This time Bigums did notice, and for a moment the smiled faltered. The fat mouse held up one paw.

"You're not one of us, Ratbane's brother. Why should we tell you anything?"

Several answers sprang to HaRed's mind. *Tira-Nor needs him. He's my brother. His family is worried to death. It's the decent thing to do.* But he knew they wouldn't respond to such arguments. After a moment, he said, "Because the truth might be good for a laugh."

Silence.

Slowly, the smile on Bigums' face expanded. "Might be," he said. "And if not, there's always the blood water. Would you like to sit down?"

10

JaRed

General Kreeg did not follow JaRed and DeStra outside, but JaRed's last glimpse of him that afternoon burned itself in his memory.

Kreeg slept among the wounded, his back propped against the mildew-fingered wall of the basement, his head tilted back, his mouth open in sleep. He looked serene; his right forepaw rested on one knee above the grimy floor.

War Claw glimmered, crooked as a beckoning finger. It twitched in the dim light of the basement, and from its tip a single drop of liquid quivered before spattering in the dust at Kreeg's feet. A familiar, deathly smell wafted through the basement.

"Well," WoKot said. "Best get on with it. Before we changes our minds, mousies."

Outside, rain fell in sheets, soaking them to the skin. Icy tendrils battered their nerves, snatched their breath away. Before long, they both shivered uncontrollably.

"Don't like the cold, eh?" WoKot sneered. "Then best get moving." He shoved JaRed in the back, probably as eager to return to the quarry as they were to find shelter from the storm.

They began to run, the exertion igniting a tiny glow of warmth deep within.

Lightning cracked in the distance, brightening the path that led them toward the White River. By the time they made it to the upturned roots of the oak tree, storm winds howled around them.

JaRed spoke over the roar of the wind. "The bridge will be treacherous in this weather. Slick. Icy. And the wind will be worse over the water. I'll go first."

DeStra's mouth drew down in a scowl that matched her tone. "I'll th–thank you to stop presuming on my g–good nature, JaRed son of ReDemec the Red. I d–don't need the help of a c-c-commoner."

"That's right, lady mousie." WoKot grinned. "You can dance across the bridge all by your lonesome. But go across you will. And you too, little runt. My orders are to see you either across or in. And I don't much care which it is."

JaRed stared.

Runt? Did the rat know that this used to be JaRed's nickname, a name he hated? Or was it just a coincidence? Come to think of it, Kreeg had called him Runt too. He shoved the thought aside as DeStra scrambled up the roots at the base of the tree. He followed her, leaving WoKot to peer out at them, the rat's head sheltered from the rain under the overhanging stump of a single root.

"Who do you think you are, anyway?" she shouted at JaRed. "Just leave me alone. Leave T–Tira-Nor alone and go away." Her gaze flicked to his forehead, eyes cold with loathing. She shuddered and turned toward the bridge.

Hopelessness washed over him. *Others have despised me before,* JaRed thought. *They've laughed at me, hated me, taunted me. But no one has ever looked at me the way she just did. What can that mean?*

The unfairness of everything that happened in the last few months brought a lump to his throat. Rejection, pure and undiluted, seeped into his pores, colder than the rain.

TaMir's words came spinning back to him from the past. *"Oh, yes, sometimes ElShua whispers a riddle in my ear. Once in a great while he may give me a hint about what will happen. But he does not tell me how. And the how, dear JaRed, is the thing that gives life color."*

DeStra padded across the rain-slicked trunk of the tree, her tail held out for balance, ladylike, with dignity.

JaRed nudged behind her, and as he left the protective backdrop of the roots, the full force of the wind slapped him in the face. Rain pelted his nose, his paws, his shoulders, stinging like cast stones as they struck. His face began to go numb.

The bridge ran slick with rainwater at either end, but in the middle, before any limb stretched out a steadying hand, its surface glittered with ice.

JaRed saw the danger immediately. In a jagged flash of lightning the dark patches of frozen rainwater reflected light at the edges. "DeStra!"

She looked back, annoyed. "Not now."

"Those black patches are ice."

She ignored him, tip-toeing carefully until she came to the first patch. Her left paw swept around in a large circle. A few more steps and she reached the first limb, clinging to it with both front paws.

JaRed took the icy area even more slowly, his breath coming in short, desperate puffs.

DeStra glanced back at him, a brief flicker of lightning high overhead outlining her face. She turned away and reached for an ice-covered limb, fingers outstretched. Her rear paws slipped. She leaned forward, wavering as the gap between her fingers and the branch widened. Slowly she began to slide over the rounded wooden horizon.

JaRed scrambled for the limb, scissored it with his rear legs, and reached out with both front paws.

The bridge rose up and smashed his jaw, sent stars whirring before his eyes.

TEN

He caught her ankle with his right paw. Her weight wrenched his back and legs. Her arms flailed the air.

Lightning.

Her arms, her eyes. Her face wet and cold and terrified.

Pain seared JaRed's spine. He was being torn in half.

Streaks of white light veined the black bowl of the sky, the gray clouds, the slashing rain.

She reached. Missed. Reached. Missed again.

One limb, an inch beyond her grasp. And her body moving now, swinging like a pendulum as she hung half-off, half-on the tree limb, upside down, the world above her, the universe beneath.

Once more. JaRed grit his teeth. *You can do it!*

Another fork of lightning, this one so close it ripped open the fabric of the sky.

She reached again, her right paw stiff with reaching.

She caught the limb.

The return force tore JaRed from the branch to which he still clung.

DeStra brought her other paw up and pulled herself to safety.

JaRed let go of her ankle and reached back to save himself. His paws slid fast across the slick surface. He groped for the branch. Clawed at the bark of the tree, scratched long shallow lines in the ice of the trunk as he slid over the edge and into the black nothingness above the river.

Once more lightning gouged the sky.

DeStra stared at him, the lovely dark eyes and delicate mouth. No longer haughty, wide with terror.

Who do you think you are?

11

DeStra

The river consumed him.

There was no splash. The foaming surface simply closed around him, and he disappeared.

A hollow feeling grew in DeStra's stomach. Rain pelted the surface of the bridge. A shaft of blue lightning forked through the blackening sky, revealing, at the far end of the bridge, a shadow that flickered and vanished as WoKot turned back for the quarry.

She stood alone in the Dark Forest.

She shivered. Her fur clung to her skin in icy sheets. She had never been so cold, so lost. The courage she pretended to have while in Kreeg's dungeon revealed itself now to be an imposter. It was JaRed's courage that had sustained her.

He saved my life.

This thought offended her conscience, so she cursed the forest, the cold, the rain.

She blamed the bridge for JaRed's death. She blamed Kreeg. She blamed fate.

JaRed would have died anyway!

Muddy, freezing, and half-starved, she looked no different than a commoner. This angered her, for she knew it was a petty and self-centered thought, and she couldn't help thinking it.

But this was what King SoSheth wanted, wasn't it? For JaRed to die?

He was a traitor.

No. JaRed wanted to save Tira-Nor, not destroy it. And he saved her life.

She stalked through the night, arriving at the edge of Tira-Nor just after dawn. The sentry at the Open Gate shook his head when she gave the password, his eyes narrow in disbelief. She told her story three times before a kingsguard officer allowed her to return home through the tunnels of the Greater Families.

When at last she lay huddled in her own sweet-smelling private chamber, she thought of JaRed falling into the river. His face, gazing up at her in shock.

She wept for a long time.

Later, she slipped out of her father's mansion and plunged through the Open Gate complex into the relative darkness of the Commons. She spent almost two full hours moving through the poorest section of the city, remembering what JaRed told her. A rat raid on the city's storerooms would be disastrous. Hundreds would die of starvation, most of the victims from the Commons.

In Kreeg's dungeon she had seen rats dying from the same thing that might haunt the poor of Tira-Nor. She tried to push the thought from her mind but failed.

She almost turned back.

Father had tried—and failed—to imprison her in a cage of protective guards and warm fur. But now she owed a debt she must repay.

She stopped at an entry hole in the southwest section. A modest place. The last chamber of the corridor, just as JaRed had described it.

Somewhere in the distant darkness an infant cried.

DeStra scratched at the entrance. A mouse appeared, a surprising shock of white on the left forepaw, her face the color of a walnut. She might have been twig-thin, had she not been pregnant. "KahEesha?" DeStra asked.

"Yes."

"Is Captain Blang here? I have a message from your brother."

12

JaRed

The river struck JaRed on the back like a giant fist, forcing the air from his lungs in a vice of sudden agony.

Water closed around him. A swirling curtain of black ice shoved him under, tugged him down and away.

He struck bottom, his legs dragging against rock and gravel, and something hard struck the back of his head. Then the river heaved and thrust him up, and he flew beyond the moon and stars, beyond the darkness of night into a place where the sun stayed fixed in the center of the universe like a chandelier.

The river lifted him clear of the darkness and he gulped air. He sputtered, gagged as water boiled up from his lungs. He saw, briefly, that he had been swept far downstream.

Without warning the river took hold of him again.

It grabbed his ankles and sucked him under as though he were a stone.

He flailed the water, felt the press of the current at his back, twisting him, tumbling him across the watery floor. Disoriented, he began to panic. He could not tell which way was up, which way down. He knew only the inexorable strength of the water, knew that the river would have its way.

Only when he could hold his breath no longer, when his lungs burned and his vision sparked with blood-red stars, when he knew he was already dying, only then did he give in to instinct. The pain in his lungs could not be resisted. He could not stop himself. His lungs demanded air.

He opened his mouth and inhaled death.

I'm dying. But ... why not? Who do you think you are, anyway?

JaRed. Son of ReDemec the Red.

Of the Commons.

Of the Kingsguard.

Of Tira-Nor.

A Seer?

No.

A Traitor?

No!

A king?

The stars grew brighter as he looked, their coal-white eyes flickering like ghosts in the silence of the water.

A broken tree limb, stuck fast between two boulders, struck him across the belly as the current propelled him forward. He felt no pain, was only dimly aware that his body struck a log. He hung there as the river made up its mind.

Then it kicked him up and over, into a white foaming mountain of cold spray, the sound of sound startling.

Stillness. A slow circle of current, comforting amidst the roar of water.

He did not move, even when he felt himself being lifted from the water and dragged to the bank.

Warmth and peace settled around him. He drifted under a gray sky, noticed the rain had stopped.

A voice spoke to him, but he did not answer. The words weren't clear and did not seem to matter. Warmth and peace would carry him from the cold, the pain, the darkness and confusion that had been his life. He lay on his back, staring up at the leaden afternoon sky, but seeing only stars that were now, tragically, beginning to fade.

A great weight pressed down on his chest, and his body jerked. Water spewed from his mouth. A bolt of pain ripped through him. Brought him back from the comforting pinpricks of light.

"Aliiive?" the voice said. "Astonishing!"

JaRed's lungs expanded, but the fluid was not all

gone from his throat. He choked and heaved buckets of river water onto the bank.

"Indeed. That won't do a tall."

JaRed gasped sweet lungfuls of air, warm as sunlight compared to the water. He hacked, breathed, hacked again, then settled into a long series of rapid breaths. His vision returned, and he turned onto one side to look for the first time on his rescuer.

A mouse. Middle-aged, with a bald patch at the top of the head from which a few wiry twigs of fur sprouted. No Tira-Noran, this mouse. JaRed would have remembered such a face: the long thin nose, the eyes peering down from the top of the world, the drooping ears saw-edged from some long-forgotten fight.

"Ahhh," said the mouse. "You skirted death by a whisker, old friend. You should be dead, you know. Popping up like a cork, and I lucky enough to spot you. Leftenant!" The mouse rose on his hind legs, looked around with his eyebrows drawn together in a single bushy line, and then knelt down again beside JaRed. "I daresay you've looked better. Tried to swallow the river, did you? Indeed! You know, we aren't exactly safe here in the open. Are you well enough to move?" He gave JaRed an appraising once-over, then looked left and right as though expecting company.

JaRed tried to rise, broke into a fit of coughing.

The mouse's eyebrows furrowed into an arrow

pointing down his nose. "Move indeed. If that isn't swallowing the seed before the rind! Any blind cow could see you need half a moment longer. LEFTENANT!"

He rose again in obvious displeasure, cast his gaze back and forth across the open space of the riverbank, and then shrugged in resignation. He sat next to Ja-Red and stared across the river.

JaRed felt too disoriented to get his bearings. He did not recognize this place, and did not know how far the river carried him. He might now be well beyond the farthest boundary of the Known Lands.

"The name is Gibbs. Colonel Gibbs. Fourth infantry, light, of the King's Grenadiers, West Exiter. I am most pleased to make your acquaintance. Especially under such timely circumstances. You are?"

"JaRed. Son of ReDemec."

"You won't understand, I suppose," Gibbs said. "You brought me back to my senses. I had nearly given up the quest. It all seemed so improbable. So fantastic. I was just saying to myself, 'Colonel Gibbs, you're a fool. This search began with help, was sustained by help, and depends on help from HQ. But you haven't given ElShua so much as a wink and a nod since you tipped your tail to the Double-You-E!' Which was the first sensible thought I've had since we left. Thought I'd lead my mice to the king of Tira-Nor alone, did I? Hoped to find the legendary city by myself? Ha! Without asking for help? Ha again! So I finally put in the call to HQ. Asked for nothing more than help finding my way. Someone who could take me to the king. And then. Well. You! Appearing! At my moment of crisis! That, old friend, is too ripe to be tossed aside as coincidence! Just goes to show that it's never too late for—" Gibbs blinked. "You do know the way to Tira-Nor, don't you?"

Without thinking, JaRed nodded.

"Of course you do!" Gibbs beamed. "I knew you were HQ's answer. Once you're feeling better, you can lead us to the king of Tira-Nor! Anything wrong?"

JaRed couldn't think. His brain had frozen solid again, a lump of ice. What could he say? He couldn't lead this Gibbs fellow back to SoSheth. "No," He sputtered. "I mean—"

"Splendid!" Gibbs stood and gazed up the long high bank of the river. "Dimble! Leftenant!"

Something flashed in the grass. "Suh!"

"Ah. Now we're getting somewhere. Which, unless I'm mistaken, is the idea. That would be my second, Leftenant Dimble."

A tall, athletic-looking mouse appeared on the river bank and bounded down to them. "Cunnel?" Dimble saluted, his arm as stiff as a coiled spring. He eyed JaRed with a mixed look of curiosity and distrust. Long bushy sideburns crept down his cheeks, and from his hawkish nose protruded a curved mass of braided whiskers.

"Leftenant. We have company. Take this chap back to camp. Put him in my quarters. See if you can scrounge up something for him to eat. I'm sure he's famished."

"Suh!" Leftenant Dimble said.

JaRed pushed himself up to one elbow. "Colonel Gibbs, I appreciate your kindness, but you must understand something. I do know the way to Tira-Nor. I lived there my whole life. But I can't go back. I mustn't go back. I'm not allowed to. Not yet, anyway."

"Oh," Gibbs said, his voice cold. "I see."

"No, you don't." JaRed pulled himself to his feet. Wobbly, but he could stand now. He might be able to walk a little way. "Are you sure you need to see the king of Tira-Nor?"

Gibbs picked at his teeth with the long, curved nail of his left pinky. His whiskers twitched. "Do pardon me, JaRed. Leftenant, I believe we'd better place a guard on our friend's quarters."

———∞∞∞———

Leftenant Dimble escorted JaRed up the riverbank where they were met by two wiry soldiers.

The ground beyond the riverbank rose slowly, melting into a flat, soggy meadow dotted with saplings. Around the meadow, elm and maple trees formed a high wall that ringed the clearing. The ground lay saturated with icy water.

Nevertheless, in the center of the clearing a gaudy assortment of mice stood at parade rest, their chests shoved out, their chins scraping air. Each wore braided whiskers.

Behind JaRed, Colonel Gibbs sniffed imperiously at the chill air and called out in a loud voice, "Grenadiers. I have the pleasure of introducing our new guide. JaRed, son of ReDemec. Of Tira-Nor. I expect you to show him every courtesy."

With one voice the mice responded. "Suh!"

"Cump'anhee!" Dimble barked. "Atten ... hut!"

JaRed supposed the grenadiers were standing at attention already. But now they drew themselves up to an even more formidable and imposing state of discomfort. Every chin craned skyward. Every back stiffened. Every chest inflated.

"I believe you were putting the grenadiers through the paces when I required you, Leftenant," Gibbs said. "No reason that shouldn't continue."

"Suh!" Dimble nodded, turned, twiddled his fingers for a moment. He stalked in front of the grenadiers like an unhappy schoolmarm. "Chin up there, Collins! Chest out! Thought you were going to cut down on second helpings, Windy? I've seen cows with smaller stomachs. And you, Private Flynn!"

Flynn stared straight ahead, his voice loud. "Yes,

leftenant?"

"Is that mud on your shins?"

"Mud?" Flynn's gaze flicked down, then back up. "Yes, leftenant. Mud."

"You'll have some excuse about patrolling again, I suppose."

"No excuse, leftenant."

"I should have you court-martialed, private!" Dimble continued, his scorn sounding almost like grudging affection.

"Yes, leftenant."

"Don't think I won't."

"No, leftenant."

"It happens, bully for you, that with Major Simmerson gone we are one officer short of the three required by regulation for that particular legal proceeding." Dimble screwed his face into a mask of disgust.

"Very good, leftenant."

"Very good, yes. For you. Bad, no doubt, for the grenadiers." Dimble sighed. "Well. Don't let it happen again."

"No, leftenant."

Dimble moved on, finding other faults that were invisible to JaRed even when pointed out. At last Dimble turned and snapped another coiled-spring salute to Colonel Gibbs. "Suh! With apologies. Able Company."

"Thank you, leftenant." Gibbs beamed. "Well, Ja-

Red? What do you think?"

JaRed looked at the stony grenadiers, erect as statues in the icy water of the meadow. "The kingsguard doesn't drill as well. Can they fight?"

Gibbs seemed to swallow something sour. His face flushed a deep violet. "Indeed."

"I meant no offense. It's just that—"

"Yesss?"

"Well, I can't help wondering why you're here. You said someone sent you? But who?"

Gibbs stood with his back ramrod straight, his chin quivering. "Upon my word, I thought I explained that. Leftenant!"

"Suh!"

"Explain our mission."

Dimble turned to JaRed but did not look him in the eye. Instead, his gaze swept past him, focused on a point someplace in the distance. "We are volunteeuhs. Following the Cunnel. Following orduhs."

Dimble apparently thought this explanation ought to suffice, for he offered nothing else.

JaRed said, "And ... ?"

Dimble frowned. "Orduhs. From HQ. We're to find the king of Tira-Nor and enlist in his suhvice. Or die trying."

JaRed's gaze slid from Dimble to the grenadiers. Still standing at attention in their neat rows.

"That was nine weeks ago. So here we are. Orduhs.

Wouldn't want to disappoint the Cunnel, would we? And we mustn't let down HQ."

"But why have you been ordered to enlist in the service of King SoSheth?"

"SoSheth? Is that his name?" Gibbs turned and gave JaRed a thoughtful look. "I imagine his majesty has gotten himself into a fair bit of trouble. Anything else, and he wouldn't need grenadiers, would he?"

JaRed's face burned. He was forgetting something important, but his mind refused to focus. A sudden desire to sit swept all other thoughts from him. "So then, you are ... you are ElShua's answer." He felt dizzy. His voice sounded far-off and unreal in the cold air. "ElShua's ... answer ... to the ..."

"Are you all right?" Gibbs asked.

But the world was tipping, sliding away. JaRed decided to rest for just a moment, but his legs were numb. He dropped awkwardly to his knees and then fell backward.

Overhead, the sky spun in lazy circles around the sun, an old dog chasing its tail.

13

JaRed

Paws raised him, carried him to a vast bowl of trees, oil-black against the sky. Under an elm the grenadiers stopped. Crawled beneath a rotten log peeling wide flakes of bark as stiff as paper. JaRed was pulled into a hollow place large enough for the whole company.

Voices sang of death and cold and battles fought long ago.

He drifted, carried on dark waters.

Periodically, someone shook him awake, offered him food he could not eat.

Fever consumed him. He lost all sense of time and place, wandering in and out of consciousness and through the murky realms of dreaming. Sometimes he thought he lay again in Kreeg's dungeon, and the old, familiar nightmares returned. More than once the scream returned too—a long, terror-stricken sound like talons rasping granite.

Often, he heard voices, surreal in the dim light, and yet close enough to penetrate the fog of unreality with warmth and life.

Once, he thought Colonel Gibbs whispered a word in his ear, but later suspected he only dreamed it.

The fever left briefly, returning what seemed mere hours later. Gibbs sighed among the grenadiers, passing the time with a honey-smooth voice that wore away the hours and unified the days into one chunk of immeasurable time.

"A story, Cunnel! Give us a story!"

"Yes, Cunnel, a ripper!"

"You lads aren't particular then?"

"How 'bout the badger?"

"The badger? Are you sure?"

A chorus of voices. "Suh!"

"All right, then. But don't complain to me if Dimble is grumpy in the morning."

Barely audible, a whisper, "Leftenant's always grumpy in the mornin'."

Gibbs drew a deep breath. "This took place long ago, before the planting of the world. In those days ElShua's garden stretched unfurrowed across the rolling hills of heaven. A vast sea of wild, untamed life. At its heart, a palace built of white stones cut the sky and separated cloud from cloud.

"Often ElShua walked among the growing things, talking to the animals who lived in the fields, the woods, the tangled roots of the mountains. He knew their names. He knew their children. He knew their hopes and dreams, their passions and secret longings. And each animal he touched went away knowing it owned a purpose in the wild lands, and its purpose was good."

JaRed shut his eyes and tried to imagine ElShua in a form small enough, close enough, to touch his head. It was a nice story, and he wanted to believe it. But hadn't he learned better? Didn't he know by now that everything wasn't part of some grand design?

"But one animal never came when ElShua called for him. His head was not touched. His ears were not scratched. His passions were not shared.

"Wroth, a rodent with a nose like a needle and eyes as black as ink, hated ElShua. His shadow trailed the footprints of the Maker, sniffing and scheming through the Wild Lands, his ears twitching as each animal was named in secret. The wolves, the opossums, the deer, the bison, the antelope. The names of their children.

"When ElShua left a home, Wroth's shadow appeared in its doorway. His voice rippled like slow poison in ElShua's wake. 'ElShua,' he would say, 'is using you. Magicking you. Twisting you. Stay away from him and you will see. Stay away from him and you will understand. His voice will lose its power. Before long you won't care whether you hear him or not. You won't need him anymore.'

"Some of the animals listened to Wroth. And in time his words worked destruction.

"The animals who stayed away did change. To them, ElShua's voice did lose its power. Before long, as Wroth had predicted, they didn't care to hear the Maker's voice any more. They no longer needed him.

"One by one they forgot their names. And when they forgot, Wroth spoke new words to them. He gave them new names, names of his own choosing, names that suited his purpose. He did this slowly; the eons went grinding along, and Wroth was subtle. Bit by bit, new identities emerged. Rabbit became Leaf-Eater. Cow became Trampler. Wolf became Stalker.

"They were not happy. They wept for loneliness. They despaired for their lost purpose. They raged at the emptiness of the universe. They hated the sound of ElShua's voice, for it reminded them of a happier time, an innocent time, a lost time.

"Among them, rumors of a violent rebellion spread. Secret counsels were held by moonlight. Whispered plans were made through lips parted in snarls. When the time was right, they would destroy the other animals, tear down ElShua's palace, and rid the universe of their awful memories. They would make Wroth the Liberator their king.

"But one Lost Soul among them began to have second thoughts."

"The badger," Flynn said.

JaRed opened his eyes.

Collins jabbed an elbow into Flynn's side. "Shhhh!"

"I'm right, though. It was the badger."

"Let the cunnel tell the story, you great lummox."

"Private Flynn is quite right," Gibbs said. "It was the badger, whose black fur was tipped with silver. He hid himself in a thicket and turned his loneliness over in his mind like a nut he couldn't crack. *I once was happy*, he thought, *but now I am sad. What is the difference?*

"Happy.

"Sad.

"A riddle. A terrible puzzle created by Wroth the rodent, who had once been the badger's friend.

"And every time he asked himself the question, 'What is the difference between happy and sad?' he ended with the same answer.

"'I don't know who I am. I have forgotten.'

"On a sunlit morning when the dew sparkled on the great trunks of trees and water laughed in a nearby brook, the badger made up his mind. He was always slow to decide anything, but now he knew that he must hear his old name again. He would return to the white palace and knock at its ivory gates.

"He had made his way back through the wild wood

to the roots of the blue-hazed mountains when Wroth, riding the neck of a great grey wolf and accompanied by a whole wolf pack, called to him.

"'Ho, Mouse-Bane!'

"The badger stopped. He did not like the hungry look in the eyes of the wolf-pack. 'Yes?'

"'Where are you going?'

"Briefly, the badger explained. He ended by saying, 'If ElShua cannot remember my old name, then perhaps He will give me a new one. For it has been long since this badger was happy.'

"But Wroth sneered. 'You must not go back to ElShua's palace.'

"'Why not?'

"'He will only magick you again.'

"'Very well.' The badger shrugged. 'If I must be magicked to be happy, then perhaps it was for magic this badger was made.'

"'You'll regret this.'

"The wolves growled and bared their fangs.

"Surrounded, the badger saw that he had been tricked. Wroth never intended good for him.

"This is of course the story from which the mice of West Exiter derive our ancient saying, the rat showed his teeth, referring to that moment when a false friend stops pretending to be nice."

"Like Flynn, right?" Collins said.

"Shut your yap, skinny."

Gibbs ignored the interruption and continued, paws clenched behind his back, his gaze distant, as though the grenadiers were not even there. "The badger fought bravely that day. And many a wolf limped away from that fight glad the odds were weighted so heavily in their favor.

"The badger lay very still, his eyes on the white cream clouds drifting overhead.

"Few of us can understand the greatness of the badger's suffering, for he did not die. None of the animals of heaven could die then. His body lay torn into bloody strips on the floor of the Wild Wood.

"Day after day Wroth sent the other Lost Souls to look at the badger in his misery. 'This,' he told them, 'is what will happen to you if you try to go back.'

"The badger was sorry he had listened to Wroth, but sorrow didn't ease the pain. His only consolation was the thought that now he knew the truth. And in his heart he pitied the other animals who had been deceived.

"Finally, after all the Lost Souls had appeared, Wroth pressed his snout against the badger's shredded left ear. 'Even now,' he whispered in a tone like honeyed poison, 'I can make you well again. You need only say the word. Curse ElShua, and you shall be whole.'"

Gibbs took a deep breath, as though to let the words sink in.

JaRed imagined Wroth's snout pressed against his ear, whispering words of treason and cowardice. He turned on his pallet and tried to thrust the image from his mind.

"Meanwhile, outside the palace, ElShua dug a well. Its waters ran deep and clear, and around its mouth he fashioned a stone wall as white as the desert sand. Next to the well he built a forge for shaping metal. The fire of its furnace burned as silver-bright as the moon and threw sparks like fireflies when ElShua's hammer struck steel.

"For eleven days and eleven nights the sound of the hammer banged through valley and field, wood and desert. The sound could be heard as far away as the mountains from which ElShua had drawn the iron he now shaped.

"The badger heard the sound as he lay in agony at the feet of the mountains. It was a lovely sound, like fingertips on the ears, but it hurt to hear because he was so alone.

"On the morning of the twelfth day, the sound of ElShua's hammer ended, and a new visitor stooped over him. A voice spoke, as gentle as a summer breeze. The agony of the badger's broken flesh was caressed by a sensation like cold water flowing over a burn. 'Mortecai,' the voice said.

"Peace enveloped him. Great hands reached under him, gathered the quivering strips of his flesh into massive palms, and carried him away from the mountains and into the Garden. And all the while the voice spoke. 'Mortecai, Mortecai, Remember.'

"The badger remembered. His name was Mortecai.

"Into the garden forge ElShua carried him. Heat blasted the badger's face from the great furnace, but he no longer felt any pain. 'You came,' he whispered.

"'It was time.'

"'Time?' He gasped. Worse than seared nerves was the torment of this word, for it wakened a resentment hidden deep in his heart. ElShua should have come sooner. ElShua could have ended his suffering days earlier—or even prevented it in the first place—but didn't. 'I waited twelve days.'

"ElShua paused over the flames. 'Would it hurt less if I told you I wanted all the Lost Souls to see Wroth for what he really is?'

"Mortecai remembered the animals coming one by one to gape at his agony. He looked into the Maker's eyes and shook his head. 'No. But it is enough that you came at last.'

"'You showed me great loyalty,' ElShua said. 'You chose truth when a lie would have served you better. You chose pain when you could have chosen safety. Because of this, I will trust you with power. I will make you the greatest of my wild creatures. I will put the power of death in your claws and teeth. No one shall be able to stand before you. Because you have suffered greatly for the sake of love, I will trust you to love greatly, and to temper your power with compassion.'

"'This is why I suffered?'

"'This is the good that will come from your suffering.'

"Then ElShua placed Mortecai into the new body he had fashioned for him in the forge. Strong as steel, as light as air, and still burning with the white heat of the furnace. When ElShua lowered him into the well, steam rose in vast clouds, hissing in the morning sunlight.

"Mortecai stepped ghostlike from the rising mist, his body floating like a feather from the wings of the Great Owl. His eyes were luminous as moons, his silver-tipped fur as soft as innocence.

"ElShua said, 'Go now and find the Lost Souls. Find them, and bring them in. Because of Wroth there are now two kingdoms. And all must choose one or the other.'

"Thus was Mortecai born anew. The Shadow-Walker, the Storm-Bringer, the Ghost-Badger."

Silence hung in the air for a long time. Gibbs stood motionless, staring into the darkness.

At last, Corporal Ryk let out a terrific yawn. "I love that story."

<hr>

THIRTEEN

JaRed woke to sunlight.

Colonel Gibbs passed in front of the entry hole and looked down. Shards of light drifted around him like tiny feathers, clung to his fur, matted the tufts below his chin and the ragged banners of gray above his elbows. He shook himself, showering the hollow with splinters of whiteness that faded to gray against the rotting mulch of the floor. "Snow," he said. "Can you believe it?"

JaRed yawned.

"Awake, are we? And coherent, no less?" Gibbs pressed one paw to JaRed's forehead. "Well, now. The fever's gone. You've been dull company the last few days."

"How long have I slept?" JaRed's throat felt like sandpaper.

"Three days. Here. Eat something." Gibbs offered a small collection of seeds. "Not much, I'm afraid, but it'll do you good."

JaRed gulped the seeds quickly.

Gibbs stroked his chin. "I think we must understand one another. I have no wish to make you an enemy. But I must convince you to help us find the king of Tira-Nor."

It occurred to JaRed that he had been pulled to safety on the south side of the river. To get back to Tira-Nor they would have to cross the river, and he knew only one way to do that. "If I refuse?"

Gibbs shrugged. "I will use force if necessary. But I believe you were sent, and that is not something to be ignored. I asked for help from HQ, and you are my answer."

"Are you certain?"

Gibbs looked at him for a long time. "No. To be quite honest, you don't look the part. But then, that's usually how it is with HQ, isn't it? Or don't you believe in ElShua?"

"I don't know what to believe anymore."

"Then why run away? What law did you break? What have you done, or left undone?"

"I broke no law." JaRed did not want to tell the story of TaMir's prophecy, of SoSheth's intense jealousy, of his own capture by General Kreeg. But he felt he owed it to the colonel. After all, something evil was stalking Tira-Nor. If Gibbs really meant to find SoSheth, he ought to know what he was getting into.

After JaRed told his story, Gibbs said, "I see. Well, you are very convincing. But it doesn't change my position. I have been sent to the king of Tira-Nor. I am obliged to take care of you as a fellow gray-whisker in need. But I am also obliged to turn you over to your king."

14

Blang

SoSheth nosed into the tiny guard chamber and leaned against the smooth clay of the wall.

Captain Blang bowed. No visitors had been allowed since his arrest. "My lord," he said.

The Cadridian guard cast him a baleful look and retreated to the tunnel.

"I have been thinking about what happened in TaMir's chamber," SoSheth said. "About the circumstances. About your lengthy service to myself and to Tira-Nor."

Blang studied the king's face for some sign of regret. Seeing none, he looked down. Better to gaze at the floor than this strange mask.

"It would be foolish to waste your talents. Foolish to keep a guard at your chamber. You who have served me honorably. You whose faithful honesty I treasure."

"Honesty?"

"I am here because you have my trust. I am willing to forget what happened in TaMir's chamber. In fact, I have decided to promote you."

"I don't understand."

SoSheth jabbed a finger to the southeast. "The Commons lacks a sufficient defensive force. With the ranks of the kingsguard depleted, I wish to bolster the militia. Transfer some of the less complicated duties to civilians. Gate-watch, for instance."

"Is that a good idea?"

"They will need training. Discipline. Who better to give it than Captain Blang of the kingsguard?" SoSheth stared out the chamber hole as a scowl twisted his face. "I considered giving my son this responsibility, but, alas, he has proven himself to be more a fool than even I suspected."

"JoHanan is no fool."

"He sympathizes with the runt."

Many sympathize with the runt. Anger stirred in Blang's gut, boiling impatiently for release. "What does this have to do with me?"

"I am giving this responsibility to you. From now on you shall be Colonel Blang. Master of the Militia of Tira-Nor."

"It is not a job for me."

"On the contrary, the job is yours already."

FOURTEEN

It was a humiliation. A demotion. A confirmation of Blang's failure. He looked up into SoSheth's cold, expressionless gaze. *What will you do when the voice of ElShua is gone?* "Find someone else, Majesty."

Blang expected rage. Another blow to his face. He would not resist the King's punishing wrath. Indeed, he would welcome it.

I deserve to die. I should have fought to save TaMir.

But SoSheth only sighed and turned, his face back-lit by haze from a glowstone in the tunnel. "You resent me. I see that. But someday you will understand."

"I will never understand murder, my lord."

"Thus, you will never be a king."

Blang opened his mouth to speak, realized he had nothing else to say.

"Besides, Colonel Blang, you have your family to think about. KahEesha. The new child. I would think you could find satisfaction in serving the Commons as militia commander if only to ensure the safety of your loved ones."

He's threatening to kill Kah! Blang whispered, "Safety?"

"I expect you only to do your duty."

For a moment, he battled the urge to spring at SoSheth and tear at his throat. Fury battled fear. His paws shook. His knees shook. The rage boiling in his gut expanded and threatened to spill over into blood.

At last he said, "Of course, Majesty."

SoSheth started to leave, then turned back. "There is one more thing I want to say to you. For the benefit of our ... friendship."

"Yes?"

In the light of the tunnel, SoSheth brushed a piece of unseen lint from the fur of his chest. "I forgive you."

15

JaRed

They left at dawn. Sandwiched between Gibbs and Dimble, JaRed was surprised at how efficiently the grenadiers marched. They spread out in groups of three, blending into the landscape more skillfully than a kingsguard patrol.

In the early evening they slid into the clearing west of Kreeg's quarry. The concrete block structure rose from the earth like a stone. JaRed stared at it for a moment before melting back into the surrounding brush.

They gave Kreeg's sentries wide berth, crossed the bridge without incident, and camped under the thorny cover of a brier patch a half day's march from Tira-Nor.

Even under the protective cover of the Dark Forest, JaRed didn't sleep easily. Something more deadly than rats lurked in the darkness. Something wild and unpredictable. Over and over his thoughts returned to the story of the Ghost Badger. He was convinced that Gibbs meant for him to hear the story. But why?

He lay awake, shivering beneath the stiff web of a rose bush as Private Collins' doleful snoring grew steadily weaker beside him. Then he drifted off, and the faces of mice began to take shape as if in a cloud, and someone shook him.

He woke from the nightmare with fear crackling in his bones, racing the length of his spine.

Gibbs peered at him in the gloom. "Can't be helped. I need to show you something."

JaRed rose and followed the older mouse past the sleeping hulks of grenadiers.

Gibbs led him to a small clearing. In the stillness of the early morning, the air felt as cold and hard as granite. His voice rose as they walked out of earshot of the grenadiers. "One of my scouts found him. From your descriptions, I thought, well. It might possibly be the same mouse."

He stopped under long shadows. A motionless form stretched out on the ground. A horrible stench befouled the air.

TaMir's corpse lay on its side. The wrists and ankles were lashed together, the body positioned unnaturally, even in death. White fur lay flat against the rounded elbows and knees.

JaRed gasped, sank slowly to his knees.

FIFTEEN

ElShua, where are you?

Gibbs read his expression and nodded. "I suppose there's no point in dragging you to Tira-Nor with us. Not if your king is capable of this."

———⚬⚬⚬———

They dug the grave together.

Just before dawn JaRed patted the mounded earth and sat back, his paws numb with digging. He did not notice the grenadiers gathered around him until Leftenant Dimble spoke.

"Where will you go, Suh?"

JaRed looked up. After a long pause, he said, "North. To the outlanders. The mice of the north meadows."

He rested his palms on his thighs and looked at the cloud-streaked sky. It was almost noon. He would not reach RuHoff's cave by sundown, but he didn't care. His anger at King SoSheth ebbed to a cool hatred that would carry him through weariness, through the night.

"Are you sure you'll be happy there?" Gibbs asked.

"They're known for their good humor. Where can I be happy if not among mice who know how to laugh?"

"Laughter can be deceiving."

"Maybe so. But happy or not, I will go to them. Maybe I can get their help against whatever is hunting Tira-Nor. At the very least, I need some answers."

Gibbs sighed. "One answer I can give you. I'm sorry, JaRed. There is more tragedy here than you know. Much more."

"What do you mean?"

"I recognize the style of the killing. The way Ta-Mir died. This is the work of Cadridians."

"ThuBrik," JaRed said. "YaGo. RahUlf. The same mice who arrested me. King SoSheth took a dozen of them into his service in the kingsguard."

"No one knew what they were?"

JaRed shook his head. "They came as emissaries."

"Cadrid does not send emissaries, JaRed. They send spies. Servants of Wroth. Slave traders. They're planning to enslave Tira-Nor."

16

SoSheth

"So." King SoSheth glared at the thirty mice arrayed before him. "The runt is alive, after all. Where is he now?"

They stood in the palace hall, their backs straight, their faces expressionless. Presenting themselves as some sort of gift, as though the king of Tira-Nor were in trouble and needed assistance.

"Well..." The leader, calling himself Colonel Gibbs, stammered in an irritating, high-brow accent. "We don't know. Wasn't part of our mission. HQ ordered us to help the king of Tira-Nor, and ... well ... here we are. At your service."

"But you met him?" SoSheth asked. "He's alive?"

"Yes."

"Where is he, then? When did you see him last?"

"Not far from here. Though, of course, we aren't familiar with the territory ..."

SoSheth's temper kindled. "By the Owl, Colonel! I expect answers, not evasion! Did ElShua send you or not?"

"He did."

SoSheth took a deep breath and spoke slowly. "Where did you see the runt last?"

"Half a day's march west. At the grave of the Seer, TaMir."

"At the what?" SoSheth rose and stumped to the end of the dais.

"At the grave, majesty." Gibbs looked up, his chin erect. "Yesterday we found a corpse due west of Tira-Nor. It was all white, and I knew it to be the body of the renown Seer, TaMir. I deemed it honorable to give the old mouse a decent burial."

"You deemed?" SoSheth spoke through clenched teeth. "And who are you? TaMir was a traitor. I ordered his body be left above ground in death as a reminder to my subjects of the price of disobedience."

YaGo, who stood in the shadows to one side, said, "Perhaps Colonel Gibbs was ignorant ahv the decree."

SoSheth stared at Captain YaGo, then turned back to Gibbs. "Is that it? You buried him because you are ignorant?"

"I am ignorant beyond excusing, Majesty."

SoSheth glanced around the room. This Gibbs fellow was no friend. He continued to give evasive answers. He walked as though he owned the ground beneath his paws. He spoke as though he carried ElShua's voice in his ear. "And what of Runt?" SoSheth asked. "How did he manage to escape thirty of you? Do you blame that on ignorance as well?"

"He did not escape," Gibbs said. "I let him go."

It took a moment for SoSheth to recover himself. Then he bellowed his rage at the domed ceiling, "GET OUT! AND NEVER COME BACK!"

17

JaRed

"JaRed? Is that you?"

He recognized the voice that spoke to him as he entered RuHoff's cave. "Yes, HaRed. It's me."

Paws gripped his shoulders. His brother stared at him for a long moment. "What happened to you?"

"Too much. I'll tell you later."

"But you're—"

A mouse shoved JaRed from behind, pushed him past a group of silent outlanders and deeper into the gloom of the cave. "Come on now, quit stalling."

He stumbled forward to the fat mouse at the back wall, the one they called Bigums.

"Says he wants our help," someone said. "Wants to join us."

"Does he?" Bigums scrutinized JaRed as he approached. "And why should we take you in, Ratbane? What do you offer us?"

"I can fight."

"Any idiot can fight. Even a rat. You'll have to do better than that."

"I killed GoRec."

"Oh, ho!" Bigums squealed. "So you're offering us another mouth to feed. And what we get in return is the fat head that comes with it? A reputation? SoSheth already despises us. If we help you, he'll kill us all."

"He doesn't have the mice for that. He wouldn't leave Tira-Nor defenseless."

"Says you."

"Yes."

"Not good enough."

JaRed looked to HaRed for help, but his brother shrugged as if to say, *I couldn't get through to him either.*

"Tira-Nor needs you," JaRed said.

"Ha!" Bigums eyes rolled back and he chortled to himself while the other outlanders chattered in the shadows. "Needs us? But isn't that why we're here, instead of wintering with our kin above the Wall? Tira-Nor's in trouble, and we don't want to miss out on all the fun!"

JaRed might have left then, but something about the fat mouse's expression stopped him. He had the feeling he was being toyed with. Tested. And Bigums was right. JaRed was asking to eat from their supplies all winter when he had done nothing to help them gather those supplies in the first place. "What do you want?"

The smile on Bigums face grew. "We haven't seen you so much as grin since you arrived. And your brother there clearly has never laughed in his life. What we want, JaRed Ratbane, is entertainment."

He stared at Bigums in silence.

"We've concocted a little test. HaRed Glumface over there refused to take it. Said he wasn't interested in being an outlander." Bigums stood and waddled over to a place on the wall where water trickled in a narrow stream to a crack in the stony floor. "This is blood-water. Poisoned. You drink it, you die." He stooped and picked up a mouse skull and held it up for the group to see. "This here's the last poor devil to fail the test. Curled up and died on the spot."

JaRed eyed the skull dubiously.

Bigums' gaze rolled sideways from the skull to Ja-Red, and then back to the skull. He heaved an enormous sigh. "Poor mum."

Laughter. Hoots from the small collection of outlanders, who edged closer.

Bigums grinned wolfishly. "A riddle is all we ask."

"A riddle?"

"The answer to a riddle, to be more precise." Bigums pointed at the etchings carved into the cave walls. "I've spent years trying to decipher these pictures. Most of my life I've strained at them, and still, I've only succeeded in one corner. Over there. Out of all that's here I've only detangled one little riddle. But not the answer. I don't know the answer. None of us does."

"All right." JaRed sniffed. "What is it?"

"Now wait a minute." Bigums held up one paw. "I said we want entertainment. The answer has to be fun. There must be a risk."

"If I can't give you the answer, I drink the blood-water?"

"And die a tragic hero." Bigums sighed in mock sorrow. "Sad, sweet fate! But we'll toast your honor every time Scrounger breaks wind."

"Forget it," HaRed said.

JaRed glanced at the skull in Bigums' hand. "What's the riddle?"

"JaRed, no!" HaRed reached for his arm.

Bigums closed his eyes, his lips curling before he spoke.

"I am gold that isn't spent.
  Never hammered, shaped or bent,
      though sometimes stretched too thin,
  I'm bought with pain
      from queens who reign,
  While kings and paupers take me in."

JaRed concentrated. The silence stretched into a long moment.

Bigums laughed. "You've noticed by now that we don't have a king here, Ratbane. No great families, no

123

commoners, no peons. No opportunity to advance."
He motioned with one paw in demonstration. "We're
all equals."

"Equals?"

"Yes."

"But you give the orders?"

"No one else wants the responsibility."

JaRed reached out, let the blood-water drip over
his palm. Ice cold, barely above freezing.

"Well?" Bigums asked, his smile ballooning.

In one swift motion JaRed drew his cupped palm to
his lips and drank.

Bigums gasped.

Silence fell.

The water tasted sweet.

"Honey," JaRed said. He looked around. "The answer is honey. And the only thing poisonous in this
room is your sense of humor."

When the laughter died away, Bigums asked, "How
did you know?"

"You have the skull, but no spine. No ribs, no
limbs, no other bones." JaRed paused. "Besides, Ta-
Mir used to come here when he was young. He drank
the same water. I decided the worst it could do would
be to make me fat."

Bigums' laughter was interrupted by a voice calling
from the opening of the cave. "Bigums! Outlanders!
King What's-His-Nose is coming with two hundred

mice!"

Bigums shot JaRed a contemptuous look and flung the skull to the floor. He wiped his paws together as though removing a layer of dirt and headed for the mouth of the cave. "Back to the Wall! Every mouse for himself!"

18

SoSheth

The rain started as a cold sputter, pattering at first against the bare branches of the trees, then turning to a steady, rhythmic drizzle that grew colder as the day went on.

King SoSheth hated rain, especially when it came in freezing bullets that slashed the ears and stuck in clumps to the fur. But he would not be deterred. The runt was out there somewhere. Almost within his grasp.

He stopped at the roots of an elm that shed its skin in tan and ochre chunks, and waited for his kingsguard to catch up. Two hundred mice made a long and awkward train, made worse by the weather, for they marched with their eyes down. If they resented this trek they kept quiet about it. No doubt they sensed his foul mood.

Colonel Gibbs and his idiotic grenadiers had

thrown SoSheth into a mortal temper. But they had, at least, brought news, even if they hadn't meant to. SoSheth knew where the runt was. He would crush JaRed and that pathetic band of outlanders under the same hammer-stroke.

Today, perhaps.

"Get YaGo," he said to the nearest mouse.

Rain blurred the north meadows, washed the dark browns and flinted hills in dull gray sheets. Was the air growing even colder? Yes. It was. He could see his breath now. And the rain spiked down in darts, collected in frozen pellets, eroding his patience.

He might have known. Winter never relaxed its grip so early. The storm had been a mere interlude, a pause before the really cold temperatures struck. Fate would first batter him with hunger and disease, then tease him with a thorough drenching, then crush him with air that stung like cold steel.

YaGo appeared at last, wearing a half-smile. "My Lawd," he said, "there is news."

"Good. Out with it."

"Scouts report a band ahv outlanders an hour's march north. It seems they are leaving RuHoff's cave."

"What direction?"

"Into the Dark Forest."

"And the runt?"

"With them."

"Can we cut them off? Keep them in the open?"

YaGo shook his head. "No. But we'll overtake them in the trees by tomorrow afternoon."

"Tomorrow." SoSheth spat. By the Owl! He would make JaRed pay. "Yes. Good. Tomorrow we'll cut them to ribbons."

YaGo smiled.

19

JaRed

They ran through the afternoon. Storm clouds pelted the outlanders with brittle white granules that clung to the fur while melting against the skin.

Their line scattered over the meadow as they ran, but JaRed occasionally glimpsed an outlander before or behind him. HaRed ran beside, easily keeping pace with JaRed's weary stride.

It occurred to JaRed that he was acting on blind and desperate faith. The outlanders boasted of a winter fortress within the Dark Forest, north and east of the Known Lands. It was, as far as he could tell, a chapel built above some kind of stone wall. What made the place a fortress was the single crack that split the wall. The crack could be climbed, but only one mouse at a time.

Bigums had made his invitation plain before he

darted away. "You're both welcome, if you can make it. We don't fight. We don't risk our necks for each other. And we won't look back for you. If you make it to the wall and up the crack, you'll find friendly faces greeting you. If not, maybe I'll write a song about you."

Later, as moonlight sharpened the edges of the trees in the distance, Bigums's voice carried back on the wind, as sad and lonely as the freezing rain. "Every ... mouse ... for ... himseeelllf!"

At sunset they reached the edge of the Dark Forest. The sky over the meadow yawned above them, freckled by starlight and then disappeared in a basket of branches. JaRed had never been this far north inside the Forest. He slowed down to pick his way through the undergrowth.

He looked back over the meadow. Several mice—perhaps as many as ten—still lagged behind them. In the distance, a long line of black dots snaked across the fields. King SoSheth and the kingsguard.

They were gaining.

Worse, the difficulties of the Dark Forest worked to SoSheth's advantage. Throughout the night, JaRed found himself having to double-back to find the passage marked by Bigums and the outlanders who had come this way earlier.

Twice after daybreak they met other outlanders stumbling on to the east. JaRed asked for help, but each time the reply was the same. "Every mouse for himself."

Each time with a snarl.

By noon the kingsguard was so close JaRed could smell their advance scouts on the wind.

They sped on through shadows deepening around him, blotting out the sun in the black-lace curtain of the trees. Cold air stabbed his lungs, cracked in his throat, burned his ears and nose with its cold-heat.

When they stopped again, he spoke with difficulty. "We have to be ... close ... to the wall."

HaRed nodded, gulping air.

"If not ..."

"If not," HaRed said, "then I can tell the king ... what I really think of him." He took a deep breath. "I never would have believed he'd hunt us this far."

"Actually, he isn't hunting us at all."

HaRed squinted. "What do you mean?"

"I mean we need to split up."

"No!"

"You have a better idea?"

"Yes. We stick together."

JaRed shook his head. "He'll just catch us both. And those who are behind us."

"What happened to every mouse for himself?"

JaRed looked over one shoulder. "Doesn't work. That's the first thing I learned in the kingsguard. It's why Tira-Nor has survived. You have to work together."

"By splitting up?"

JaRed nodded. "I'm going to draw them away. You get to the wall with the others. I'll get there when I can." He put one paw on HaRed's arm. "And save me something to eat, will you?"

20
JaRed

Six kingsguard warriors pursued him. Fast mice. Strong mice. Determined mice.

Through shadow and brush they chased him. Crossing trail and gully, crashing through frozen bracken and snow-dusted leaves. Barely twenty paces behind. If they did not close the distance in their pursuit, neither did JaRed widen it.

He could not make out their identities, for he did not spend energy and motion in looking behind him. And though at first they shouted to each other as they ran, he could not tell from their voices who chased him.

No one wasted breath now, the only sound a sinister scuttling of paws through bracken.

The pain that knifed into his ribs early in the race subsided. Now he ran as a smooth machine. His legs blurred to numbness, his mind whirred with precision, calculating the path of least resistance, the path that would lead his pursuers to a false step. His heart whammed in his chest, forced blood through his veins, firing him against the cold.

Always he ran south. South into the dark heart of the forest, until light flashed around him and the world opened on a flat, oblong meadow of white glass and crystalline sparks.

For a moment he slowed his pace, though he did not stop altogether.

He saw a long pond, rounded at the ends like a melon, and at its edges, pellets of frozen rain. White ice pierced by stiff brown cattails, rimmed in mud and rock. A white frame encircled the pond. In its center, dull gray spoke of deep waters and hidden heat. This was the heart of the Forest. And the center of the heart still defied the cold.

Ice lay in a thin sheet on the surface. Thin enough to reflect the murky depths through its onion skin.

JaRed did not stop. For who could run as he did? Who could go where he did? The little Runt. The waste of air. The half-mouse.

LaRish, his mentor, spoke to him from the past. *"Sometimes small can be dangerous, I theenk. Like zee point of zee claw, no?"*

He shot out onto the pond, his paws scrabbling for traction on the smooth surface, and he was forced to slow down.

He risked a look back. Three mice erupted from the underbrush and onto the ice. Another followed soon after, and then two more. The leader whipped his head back and forth.

RahUlf.

Hatred rose in JaRed's heart. He remembered the beating RahUlf gave him outside the Great Hall. He remembered TaMir's body, stiff with rigormortis. He remembered Gibbs saying, "They send spies. Servants of Wroth. Slave Traders.

RahUlf's size would be his undoing.

JaRed slowed, his paws splayed wide to spread his weight across the largest possible surface.

RahUlf shouted for him to stop, but JaRed ignored the command, instead moving purposefully to-wardsthe center of the pond, sliding around and over the brown pockets of death that lurked just below his outstretched paws.

RahUlf shouted again, this time to the other mice behind him, to HaKo, MinImin, EttuNu, and two others JaRed didn't recognize. "Spread ..." he struggled to breathe. "Spread out!"

JaRed stopped. The ice trembled beneath him like a dying animal. His fingers went stiff. Vibrations skipped through the cool hard sheet, sent shivers of fear darting to his armpits.

RahUlf and the others came closer. Then they too, stopped.

"Give up," RahUlf said. "You're trapped." His voice came more gently. "Don't make this deefficult."

JaRed turned to meet his gaze. "RahUlf ..."

What would he say? *I know what you are. And I'm going to kill you just like I killed GoRec.*

No.

Besides, RahUlf was only a pawn. A puppet. The real villain was King SoSheth.

A king ought to protect his people, not hunt them.

Why did ElShua allow SoSheth to remain king? Why not strike him dead? Promote JoHanan in his place? Bring sense to a senseless world?

Why did ElShua allow evil to thrive?

JaRed sighed. "You're a good soldier, RahUlf. Loyal."

"Give up," RahUlf said. He glanced down at the surface of the pond. "Before the ice breaks."

"Loyal. But, I'm afraid, too heavy." JaRed turned and stepped forward. Over the murky brown. Over the center.

The ice shuddered, creaked, groaned. A long, withering sound like teeth grinding together hissed from the surface.

Water.

Fear raced through his belly. Against his will, he shook. He felt again the icy current of the White River flooding his lungs, holding him under, pummeling his body with its relentless fists.

He forced himself to go on.

Sleet flicked and tumbled across the pond.

He moved slowly, blinking, the wind licking his eyes to tears.

"Wait!" RahUlf raised his paw. "No. I'll follow. Ett-Unu, HaKo. Take the left side. The rest ahv you stay back."

Swirling. Cold. JaRed stared down through the surface, saw only the brown smear where sunlight reflected off the underside of the ice, bent to shadow beneath him. For a moment he hesitated, as though staring the Great Owl in the face.

I've seen you before. But I've never understood.

A piercing sensation. His paws were numb.

RahUlf's claws clicked on the surface, closer.

The spell of the water didn't last, and JaRed stepped forward. Stepped again. And again.

His paws hit a patch of snow that crunched under his weight. Beneath him, the brown faded to white. The creaking of ice came from behind him.

A sound shrieked through the emptiness, slow and ghastly and haunting. The pond opened its mouth.

The ice split, then collapsed, erupting in a blister that splintered the length of the pond. Tendrils opened and ran in ten thousand directions, forking into veins that sliced the surface into brittle flakes.

A dull plunk snapped JaRed's head around.

RahUlf disappeared.

Then several plunks, all nearly simultaneous.

Wind swept the other five mice from the ice with an open palm.

In the very center, a tiny swish of water heaved upwards, then globbed back into the fractured surface.

JaRed remembered—water delivered evil into the world. Lord Wroth, dropped from heaven by the beak of the Great Owl into the sea, rose up from the rolling waves to curse the Earth with his ignoble presence.

Wroth must have made that same sound, going under.

On the far shore more mice emerged. SoSheth. YaGo. Scores of the kingsguard.

They stopped at the frozen mud of the bank. SoSheth's eyes scanned the surface of the pond.

JaRed slid forward, toward the hole in the broken ice. He moved slowly, inexorably.

He had told them to turn back. He had warned them. Hadn't he?

He paused on ice as thin and brittle as aged paper, and glared at the mice across the pond.

Several of the kingsguard started to approach, but the king motioned them back. He stared placidly at JaRed, his face flaring in the light of dusk.

SoSheth! Whose blind stupidity and reckless lust for vengeance would not rest even with killing the innocent. The king must kill and kill and kill.

Rage licked JaRed's soul with a hot tongue. He shook with the heat of it. He wanted the king to die. Wanted it more than anything.

A sickening sense of loss overwhelmed him. Still, the rage grew. Where was ElShua? JaRed no longer trusted the old stories, the prophecies, the ancient truths.

ElShua is a lie. A fairy tale. A story for kits. And then, *But isn't that what SoSheth believes too?*

Behind him, the sun buried itself in a shroud of black trees as the shadow of the Forest crept past him.

SoSheth's countenance repulsed him. He felt nauseous. Bile rose in his throat.

The ice snicked beneath him, as though licking its lips. He looked away. Down. Into the clean nothingness of the water. Where he saw, reflected in the water, a gray sky dimming to purple.

In the settling water an image appeared. RahUlf's body, suspended midway to the bottom, looking up, his face pale.

But it was not RahUlf.

No.

Someone more familiar still.

TaMir, the old Seer, his face twisted into a scowl. Full of anger, full of spite. The prophet's face shimmered, the white fur of his head burning silver in the brown muck, as brilliant as the ice itself.

Still JaRed stared; his stomach twisted into a knot.

Another vision? A revelation like those he'd seen during the rat siege?

No.

His jaw dropped. His eyes widened. Truth broke over him slowly, like dirt falling on a grave.

The white hair. The scowl. The unrestrained fury.

Time hung upside down a moment longer, long enough for him to be sure. Long enough for the rage and hatred and unbelief to drain away, washed clean by awe.

"What has happened to you?" they all asked. First DeStra. Then WoKot and Kreeg. Not Gibbs, of course, because Gibbs had never seen him before. But then, later, the way HaRed looked at him.

As though he were mad.

A pause, a furtive look down, then back, as though staring through him.

JaRed?

Again he saw the fear in their eyes. And, of course, they didn't have the nerve to ask. None of them. No one had asked when, or why, or what it meant. And this was a strange thing, that even there on the ice, he didn't blame them. For how could they have asked the question? They didn't know that he didn't know.

The reflection in the water was his own.

He stared at himself. White fur spread in a crescent mane from the top of his head to his chest. A crown of snow. A lion's crest.

The mantle of a Seer.

No! Not this. Not white. Not me. Please. For it was hatred that fired his anger, and though the anger fled, the hatred remained.

It can't be! I want SoSheth to die!

Deep within him a voice spoke. A whisper so loud it could not be mistaken. Kindness and severity intertwining like gossamer in an unseen web. *Who do you think you are?*

21

HaRed

HaRed eventually found the Wall. It rose above the treetops as a sheer cliff. Its massive, irregular stones, mortared in broken concrete, inclined pellmell to a line of distant weeds at its crest. Here and there, a narrow drainpipe jutted from the rocks above a long scar of rust.

A crack split the wall, jagging through seam and around stone all the way from base to crown. Weeds thrust from the gap, as did occasional tufts of grass and one determined seedling that sprouted midway up.

HaRed stared up at it, awestruck. It looked like the end of the world. It was a moment before he noticed the mice scaling the crack. Outlanders. The last of the group from RuHoff's cave.

JaRed's ruse worked.

But where was JaRed?

He watched as one-by-one the mice dragged themselves upward on weary limbs. Invariably, they hesitated when they came to the jutting tree and had to swing out over nothingness by their front paws and hoist themselves up. From the top of the wall, outlanders dropped jokes and insults to prod the climbers. Their voices reached HaRed where he stood hidden in the trees. "Don't just sit there! My mother did it twice this morning, and she was pregnant. Both times!"

HaRed waited through the afternoon, until the sun leaned on the horizon so low he could not see it, though its light fired the bodies of the mice on the wall. Here he lay in the shadow of the Forest. There, on top of the Wall, on top of the world, daylight still reigned.

But where was JaRed?

The question grabbed him by the throat and would not let go. The answer was too obvious.

Two hundred of the kingsguard pursuing one mouse. Even JaRed could not survive against such odds.

Could he?

Perhaps he had found a place to hide. Perhaps he was hurt and needed help.

HaRed made up his mind in a moment, slipping away toward the black heart of the forest without a sound.

Problem was, he couldn't read a trail. Subsequently, he didn't even know where to begin looking for his brother. He only knew the direction—JaRed had gone west, toward SoSheth and the kingsguard.

But JaRed excelled at moving unnoticed, and the fading daylight left the forest in a mist of cold gloom, wrapped in shadows that drooped from the treetops and stretched from unknown to unknown.

By dusk HaRed was lost.

Brilliant. HaRed to the rescue. Hold on JaRed! I'll be there in a couple of days. Then, together, we'll fight our way through two hundred of the kingsguard and run back to the safety of the Wall.

The Wall. Which lay who-knew-where.

He stood alone in a silent cave of deepening gloom. *Stupid!*

But then, the cure for stupidity was what?

Cool reason.

This place was not so different from the alcove in the southern perimeter tunnel of Tira-Nor where he used to go to think. It was colder, of course. And more exposed.

He had tried to angle south in pursuit of JaRed, but he dared not reverse his route at this point. He didn't know how far south he had come; if he went too far north he could easily walk right past the Wall without ever seeing it. He would die in the Deep Unknown.

He retraced his steps in his mind. As near as he could tell, the sun was setting there. West.

He thought of the Wall, the crack that marked its surface, the sapling, the rusting drainpipes.

Drainpipes. Water. The shallow culvert at the base of the Wall.

He sighed with relief as the answer broke over him. JaRed had told him about a stream that divided the wood. HaRed would follow it northeast until he found the culvert. The culvert would lead him to the Wall.

But what about JaRed?

A snap broke the silence, followed by the sound of shuffling feet. Careless motion, and growing louder.

Someone was coming.

Two someones.

HaRed stood perfectly still. He heard a sound not unlike a small branch whapping into a face.

"Ow!" said a voice.

"Shut up, Bulger," said another.

Ahh. Rats!

"Shut up, he says. Shut up? Then quit hitting me in the face!"

"I'll quit hitting you when you shut up. Got that? You quit making noise and you won't get hit."

"But I didn't make noise," Bulger said, "until you hit me."

"Didn't make noise, he says. Says, mind you. For

your information, Bulger, you make noise when you walk. You make noise when you eat, when you sleep, even when you breathe. When you die, you will make more noise than a pig in a bean field. Even I can hear your fat feet. I can hear you walk with my chawed ear."

"But don't hit me, RiKit, that's all. Ow!"

"I warned you."

There came a long silence, after which RiKit said, "That's better."

More silence. Then: "All right, come on. Bulger? Bulger? Where'd you go, maggot? If you deserted, I'll have both your ears and an eye! Bulger?"

HaRed hesitated. He knew how to get back to the Wall now. He could find it by morning. And yet, the presence of the rats could not be ignored. He sensed an opportunity.

Scouts from the kingsguard had been looking for the rat hideout without success. SoSheth wasn't the only one who wanted information about Tira-Nor's enemies.

HaRed knew the prophecy. More than this, he knew his brother's heart. JaRed would be king some-day. Defender of Tira-Nor. Protector of its people. And even if he weren't, JaRed would still do every-thing he could to save the mice of the Commons.

It came down to this: JaRed would want to know where the rats were hiding.

146

TWENTY ONE

So. Perhaps HaRed's stupid heroics would not be wasted after all.

The rat stumbled off into the distance.

HaRed waited until the sound grew fainter, and then followed.

22

JaRed

He spent two hours masking his trail in the black belly of the wood. He headed upstream on the eastern slope of a frozen-banked creek that skipped its way through the Dark Forest to the White River.

In the middle of the night he stopped for a rest, exhausted. He would never make it back to the Wall tonight.

He curled into a ball beneath a rock and slept, though the cold night air crept under the stone and seeped through his fur. In an hour he awakened, shivering, wondering if he would ever sleep through the night again. But since the body needed rest, he remained still.

Despair crouched at the doorstep of his consciousness, scratching to be let in. The same thoughts twisted through his mind in an endless circle from which he felt powerless to escape, like some giant wheel spinning in a vast ocean of nothingness.

I don't even want to be king. But if I'm not made king, ElShua's promises are lies, and everything I've believed is a sham. But does it matter? I don't even want to be king!

Spinning, spinning.

The sun rose. JaRed lay in a cupped earthen palm, as motionless as the rock above him. Bit by bit, the gloom of night receded, and the black skeletal bones of the Dark Forest changed into brown and gray sticks.

Once, a deer ghosted into view. A yearling, it nibbled at the bark of a tree, head craned, tongue flicking like a dog's, the brown eyes as deep and mysterious as moons. It bolted at the sound of a cracking tree limb, its tail flashing white.

The sun continued its march across the sky.

Afternoon gave way to evening. The air grew cooler. Sunlight glinted off patches of ice and frost and then took on the orange-warmth of dusk.

Shadow melted into shadow. The trees moved closer together. A whole day of not moving.

His eyes focused on the twin puffs of warmth jetting from his nostrils. He might remain here forever, his breath growing less, his body merging with the shadow of the earth, becoming at last more dust beneath the rock.

And why not? I'm not afraid to die. Perhaps I deserve to die.

The answer presented itself wordlessly. Memories of laughter. Smiling faces. Oli. NeVin. UnDrew.

Luk and Raz.

JaRed turned in the now-warm hollow, stuck his nose into the cold air of night.

If he gave up now, the innocent ones in the Commons would have no chance of surviving the winter. SoSheth certainly wasn't looking out for them.

The air grew heavy. Silence descended over the Forest.

He squirmed from his hiding place and stood in the bright starlight that misted the shadows of trees in silver ribbons.

He saw it with his waking eyes.

For a moment his mind refused to accept its reality, the enormity of its presence.

The Ghost–Badger towered above him. Its snow-frosted fur glistened against the black ether of its body.

JaRed froze. Terror raised the fur on his back.

The Badger's head swiveled. The great snout lowered. The luminous eyes bore down on him.

JaRed stepped forward, drawn like a moth to its presence.

Bodies lay at its feet. Shattered. Blood-soaked. Mangled. He recognized them. Familiar faces all. MeerQo. HarVik. LimJik. KoVeek. Mice of the kingsguard. Friends, not long ago.

In the shovel of one paw it held King SoSheth. The king's face contorted in a mask of terror so violent that JaRed felt genuine pity for him.

Then the Badger spoke. Its voice came like ice breaking, a slow, creaking whisper that hushed all other sound and slowed the universe to a crawl. "Is this what you want?"

Shame flooded through him, followed by self-loathing. The Badger had seen through his outward shell and gazed into his true self.

Yes. This is what I want. I want those who hurt me to suffer. I want you to kill them. I want to wash myself in their misery. But please! I don't want to want it!

"There are now two kingdoms," Gibbs had said. "And all must choose one or the other."

But what if I have both kingdoms inside me?

JaRed stepped forward, his gaze fixed on the Badger's bloody claws. "Take me instead."

The Badger leaned over him, its eyes pools of fire. SoSheth fell from its grip and thudded to the earth.

Aghast, JaRed knelt. He turned his head, for he could not meet its gaze as he waited for the death blow.

The Badger's voice boomed like rolling thunder. Its body hovered in the air. "What is the worst thing that can happen to you, JaRed, son of ReDemec?"

Its voice shivered in his body as darkness drained away the light.

The fireflies vanished.

The Badger was gone.

───⊶⊷───

Distant voices brought him to all fours. JaRed retreated to the stone and listened.

The voices grew louder. Three he recognized; the others were distorted by the crashing of paws through the frost-hardened leaves of the forest floor.

"WoKot!"

"Here, boss!"

"Shut these fools up before they wake the world."

Kreeg. No doubt about that voice. JaRed would know it in his sleep.

"Right, boss. Zip it, curs!"

The voices subsided, and the sound of the rats faded into the distance, but not before JaRed counted them. Kreeg had crossed the White River again and would be making mischief before the night ended. And he had brought his entire force of rats with him.

Tonight Kreeg would launch his raid on Tira-Nor's storerooms while SoSheth and the kingsguard wandered around in the woods.

JaRed stayed under the stone for a moment longer, thinking. The irony of the situation galled him.

He couldn't stop the rat General from attacking Tira-Nor. But he could prevent Kreeg from retreating safely back to the quarry afterward. He could deliver

TWENTY TWO

the rat to SoSheth in a foolproof trap.

All SoSheth had to do was recognize it.

23

HaRed

His legs ached. His shoulders ached. His eyes ached from straining to see in the dark. His paws, which began hurting two days ago during the forced march, broke open and bled. This worried him, for the smell of blood could draw predators.

Fortunately, the rats blundered through the frosted bracken with all the discretion of terrified dairy cows, and HaRed was able to follow their trail.

Just before dawn, he came to an open space in the woods.

A hunter's cabin, long since left to rot, nestled in the clearing. Shadows striped its slat-board siding. At one end the collapsed roof leaned against a log rail that spanned the porch. The chimney, dressed in un-cut stone, still rose above the gable. It cast a long moon-shadow over an upturned washtub rusting in the yard. The end of the shadow draped a sagging outhouse, the door of which slanted now on one hinge.

A single cloud drifted in front of the moon, then moved away.

HaRed searched the darkness for some sign of the danger that stalked him here. He sniffed. It came from a memory. From a to-the-death fight. A day when he sank his teeth into a rat's throat, and his nose into its fur.

This was the same smell. The smell of rats. Of grease and rottenness and decay and death.

This must be their headquarters.

It made sense. The stories of Ur'Lugh rats who survived the Battle of JaRed's Fang. The rumors of attacks on kingsguard patrols. What better place for a rat force to re-form? The cabin provided winter shelter, perhaps even some long-forgotten store of food.

HaRed dreaded leaving the relative security of the shadows, but he felt compelled to find out for certain if he was right.

His gaze swept the clearing again. The outhouse, the washtub, the chimney. A water pump on the far side of the house, just visible through the empty space of the front porch. The shuttered windows. The gaping hole beneath the cabin, which was built on four stone pillars, and from which pieces of forgotten trash jutted. An old swing-set, a roll of chain-link fence, a bent bicycle frame.

HaRed swallowed, licked his lips, and slipped forward into the blue papery light of the moon. He moved fast, crossing the open space to the outhouse in a flash. He pressed himself against the cloak of the rotting wood exterior and waited for a sentry to sound the alarm.

No alarm came. He waited a moment longer, calculating the distance to the cabin, and decided to make instead for the upturned washtub.

He took a deep breath and plunged into the openness as though it were deep water, his heart thudding, the pain in his feet all but forgotten.

On the far side of the tub he waited again in shadow.

A voice exploded from under the cabin. RiKit's unmistakable snarl broke the silence. "All right, ladies! Wake up! And get your stinkin' hide off my sleepin' rag, Wormy! Anyone seen Bulger?"

There were disgruntled protests, bleary denials. The last traces of doubt disappeared from HaRed's mind.

The most dangerous part still lay ahead. He would have to get close enough to count the rats, get some estimate of their strength.

Of course, he could just leave now. JaRed would be grateful for the new information on the rat hideout. But more information would be required. Other mice would be sent to estimate the rats' strength.

Was this a small band? An outpost of some larger force? Or perhaps only a gathering of hunger-allies, a few rat families who joined forces in winter to steal food from the less powerful.

Other mice shouldn't have to come back here to risk their lives later. Not when he was so close.

HaRed leaned around the corner of the tub and looked, scouring the earth for the quickest, safest way. Four heartbeats would take him to the shadow of the chimney, then two to the foundation. He would listen and watch, waiting for the rats to stir under the cabin, waiting for them to give some clue as to their numbers.

On three. He flexed the muscles in his legs and took a deep breath. *One. Two ...*

He stepped into moonlight.

The alarm sounded—a long high rat-screech, a sound like a ten-penny nail scraping limestone.

The fur on HaRed's neck stood on end. He stopped, frozen by indecision.

On the far side of the clearing, dozens of rats emerged from the forest, slinking toward the cabin with ears laid back, tongues lolling, teeth bared. Their breath popped and curled like gunsmoke in the night air.

HaRed recovered and dodged out of sight behind the washtub. He pressed himself into the darkness, wondering if anyone had seen him.

"What 'ave we here?" A voice, carried on spittle, rasped in the darkness. "Somepin' niiiiiiice what to eatsy? Eh, mousey mousey mousey?"

Slowly, HaRed looked to his right.

A rat stood there, staring at him from the shadow of the washtub. Its fox-jowled face drew wide in a vicious sneer. It reached out with its front paws and circled HaRed's neck in an iron grip. "And whatsa mousey doin' watchin' the rat nasties what sleeps, eh? Watchin' for whats?"

Far behind him, RiKit hurled commands at his drowsy troops. "Up, grubs! Up, dungbeetles! Move it move it MOVE IT!"

The moon spun overhead. HaRed couldn't breathe. He felt himself lifted. His feet left the ground, kicking.

The rat's grip tightened.

He clawed at its wrists with hooked fingers, but it was like trying to shatter steel with his bare paws.

A current of fire ringed his neck. His eyes bulged. A wet gurgling sound rose within him. The edges of the world blurred under a gray haze.

"Heh heh. Soft mousey neck. Pasty eyes so cold now, eh?"

In desperation, he hammered both fists into the rat's forearms, pulling it off balance.

It staggered forward, its forehead striking the side of the washtub with a sound like a muted bell hammer. "Whatsey," it said, eyes rolling back. It tottering on wobbly hind legs, then collapsed sideways in a heap.

HaRed sucked in the cold air. He could not see. His left shoulder ached. His nose felt as though it were stuffed into a shoe.

Stars circled before him. He blinked, then realized that he was lying face down on the ground. The rat, now unconscious, had fallen against his shoulder. His nose lay pinched between the tub and the earth.

He pulled. Whiskers snapped. He staggered to his feet, heard shouting, and remembered the rats in the clearing.

He was trapped. He couldn't cross the open space to the cover of the forest without being seen. Tired as he was, he couldn't outrun so many of them. Worse, before long the rat would regain its senses and start whatseying again.

"Eh?" The rat moaned.

HaRed's gaze landed on the washtub, its spot rusted edges flaking around black holes.

If JaRed were here he would disappear. HaRed paused for a moment longer as the idea came into focus. Where would JaRed hide?

In the washtub!

He pressed his paws against the tub, felt around the nearest hole. Too small. He squinted in the darkness. Higher up gaped a larger hole, but beyond his reach.

Then he remembered Whatsey. He climbed onto the rat's back, reached up for the jagged edge, and heaved.

Flakes of metal sawed into his palms.

He held back a scream and tipped forward into the darkness. Rusty teeth bit into his left leg, but he felt no pain, only a stubborn tug.

He landed on his back. Overhead, moonlight streamed through the holes and seams in the upturned bottom of the tub.

From far away he heard a voice. "BlaKote. Come out. War Claw is here. Time for your parley with fate."

Something warm and wet spilled down HaRed's leg. He grabbed his thigh with both paws, felt the wetness there, and gasped. He bathed his glistening paws in a cool shaft of moonlight, his blood congealing to black, its smell terrifying.

In the silence, he felt, rather than heard, the mocking laughter of Lord Wroth at his side. *The Owl, the Owl. The Great Owl comes for you! Eh, mousey? And a good thing too, perhaps. 'Cause he's the onlyest one knows mousey's here.*

Then the nerves in his leg awoke, and the pain hit him, and dying didn't sound so bad after all.

24

JaRed

By the time JaRed made his way south to the bridge, clouds drifting from the west blotted the moon. In the darkness he was forced to slow down and pick his way along the high cliffs of the White River until he saw the wire-brush bristles of the tree fanning the horizon. A light breeze whispered along the forest floor, though the branches of the dead oak stood motionless where they had fallen.

He glanced over the edge of the cliff. The river no longer raged. It slid through the narrow gap and curled away in a flat ribbon into darkness.

He searched for almost half an hour before he found a makeshift path. Twice he kicked loose stones into the chasm and huddled in silence for the delayed *splunk*.

He didn't have to go far down the cliff face to find what he was looking for.

The branch he had seen on his first crossing of the river ended a few feet from the top of the cliff. The river still lay a terrifying distance below him.

The branch stabbed the rock of the cliff face, angling up into a major limb that arced halfway across the river. JaRed gripped it in both paws, measuring its girth with his fingers. If this branch were broken, the tree would fall. The bridge would be destroyed. Kreeg and his crew would have nowhere to hide, nowhere to retreat. The kingsguard could be thrown against them, and the rats would be eliminated.

If.

A new thought occurred to him. On a whim, he climbed back to the top and stared across the emptiness to the cliff on the far side. He made up his mind in an instant and leapt to the trunk of the tree.

He crossed without looking down, dropping lightly to the ground on the far side. As he suspected, no sentry stood guard there. Kreeg had emptied his reserves, brought every able body with him.

JaRed made his way to the quarry and hid himself in the darkest shadows of the basement window-well on the east side of the house. Somewhere in the distance, indistinct and forlorn, a band of coyotes howled.

JaRed took a deep breath and pushed into the darkness of the basement.

The stench of decay nearly knocked him off his

feet. He stuffed one paw in his mouth and fought back the urge to vomit.

Death.

He felt along the wall at his back. There was a way down, he knew, and he groped in the darkness to find it.

Knowing they would come for him, he drew a deep breath and said, "Is anyone here?"

Knowing they would find him. Would reach out of the inky blackness with clawed fingers and force him back into the dungeon. But he had seen the look in their eyes. The dying ones. The rat children. The rat women. They were not so very different from his own people.

Silence. No claws reached. No rats emerged to rake at him with vengeful paws.

"Please. If you're alive, say something. There is time still to get out."

He waited.

Nothing.

A picture came to mind. Kreeg, with his back against the wall. War Claw held out like a knife, gleaming. And from its cold tip, a single drop of liquid formed and fell like a tear to the dirty floor of the basement.

JaRed spent two hours in the blackness of the quarry, the death-odor churning his stomach, flaying his throat raw as he searched for the hole in the floor.

All the while a grim realization knocked at the door of his mind. The poordevils didn't die a natural death. The desk-drawer smell that still clung to them proved that.

Kreeg killed them.

War Claw killed them all.

———∞———

JaRed fled across the deserted lawn, across the bridge, across the face of the cliff's edge. He sucked in the clean cold air, tried to wash the stench of death from his throat, from his mind.

He listened to the loud, terrifying sound of water far below, and set his mind on the task at hand.

He would destroy the bridge and remove Kreeg's base of safety. He would gnaw through the supporting limb one bite at a time.

TaMir once said the greatest things in life were done by persistence, not skill or strength. In the old stories, the grains of sand were placed by the sea one by one until the shore was so vast it could not be measured.

An acorn had grown bit by bit into this massive oak, and bite by bite JaRed would remove it.

164

25

Kreeg

General Kreeg stepped into the open field. WoKot and the full strength of his raiders followed. Fifty six veteran rats, wily fighters all, and as loyal as any rat could be. But they were not enough. He needed more scrappers to execute the final stages of his plan. He was right about the runt and right about the mouse king. Such opportunity begged seizing.

The hunter's cabin loomed above them, its porch cast in shadow. He smelled the presence of other rats here and knew with certainty the reports of his scouts were accurate.

Ur'Lugh rats. Fierce but sloppy. No guard stood watch this fine night. Or else the guard on duty had fallen asleep. He would need to check into this later.

Noises erupted from the cabin. A rat cursed, its voice muffled but audible even from here: Up, grubs! Up, dungbeetles! Move it move it MOVE IT!"

Kreeg considered a surprise assault. He could wipe out the Ur'Lugh before they came fully awake, but he needed them. Even with two hundred kingsguard mice wandering the Dark Forest, and Tira-Nor's gates barely defended, his skullcrew of less than sixty fighters was too small to guarantee the success of his plan. Besides, he would rather let the Ur'Lugh execute the less tasteful elements of the attack—and bear the greatest risk.

He drew himself up to his full height and turned to WoKot. "I want four scrappers on the other side of that old washtub. Ready for anything."

"Right."

Kreeg glanced up at the stars.

A fine night for killing.

"BlaKote." Kreeg shouted. "Come out. War Claw is here. Time for your parley with fate."

BlaKote's shadow appeared in the doorway of the cabin behind a protective line of skirmishers. Kreeg considered this a positive sign. Hiding behind his rats would make BlaKote unpopular.

He leaned against the frame of the doorway. "Kreeg. I knew you'd turn up somewhere."

Kreeg stepped into the open, advancing in front of his own warriors in a wordless boast. "I've come to take your rats away from you."

BlaKote sneered. "They're not for sale."

This brought a few laughs from the Ur'Lugh. They

were dangerous rats, though they hadn't recovered from the shock of GoRec's death at the tooth of a scrawny mouse. These Ur'Lugh had pride; they wanted to believe their leader was the meanest, nastiest, deadliest fighting rat in the kingdom. And, in a way, he was.

Many an upstart rat had died at BlaKote's teeth. Among the Ur'Lugh, none moved faster, struck harder, or bit deeper than BlaKote the Shadow.

His silken fur hung on his shoulders like a streak of oil. His relaxed demeanor disguised a muscular frame and a legendary agility as lethal as that of a weasel.

But BlaKote did not have War Claw.

For just a moment, Kreeg wondered what it would be like to die, what he would see when he stepped over that threshold. Might he catch a glimpse of it if he were to stare into BlaKote's dying eyes at just the right moment?

Without warning, the old fear returned.

What if there is an afterlife?

No. You came from dirt, and when you died you went back to it. End of story.

Kreeg bared his teeth at BlaKote. "You always were a coward."

The insult made further negotiations impossible. The Law of Leadership had been invoked.

BlaKote's gaze swept over the gathered rats. Kreeg's warriors watched in expectant silence. The moon stroked the earth with long fingers of light.

The rats formed a loose circle, sizing each other up. Both skullcrews would merge, which meant a change in status. If BlaKote won, Kreeg's warriors would be absorbed as low-level scum, and vice versa.

But the blood-lust of a death match overpowered their fear. Not since the days before GoRec came to power had two well-matched masters dueled.

BlaKote descended from the porch with a kind of royal arrogance, his eyes scheming. "When this is over," he said to Kreeg's crew, "You are welcome to join us. So long as you follow orders."

"I heard you were eloquent." Kreeg dropped into a low fighting stance and waited. "I expected your last words to be more profound."

BlaKote exploded from the far side of the circle, lunging low with teeth bared, his shoulders pistoning as he drove forward, his coat a blur against the earth, his tail a streak.

Kreeg circled, drawing first blood almost by accident. A long swipe with the bared claws of his left forepaw—intended as a feint—gouged into BlaKote's chest as he came forward. Nothing serious, but it felt good.

I wonder if I could kill him without War Claw? Or have I grown soft, depended on the weapon too much? Am I the rat they believe me to be?

He made up his mind in an instant, surprised at the

intensity of his own fear. And yet he felt calm. Satisfied. Content.

BlaKote tried to drive Kreeg against the half-circle occupied by the Ur'Lugh.

Kreeg gave way against three rapid strikes from BlaKote, then a fourth, then a fifth. But he would not succumb to mere physical prowess. On the sixth strike he moved in, took a hammer-blow from BlaKote's fist, slipped underneath and reversed his stance. Pain spiked down the side of his face to his neck. A burning sensation, fired by blood.

Kreeg's move caught BlaKote by surprise. He gripped BlaKote's right forelimb in his own left paw, struck upward with the point of his right elbow into BlaKote's exposed ribs, and was rewarded by the muted crack of a bone snapping.

BlaKote's breath came out in a gasp.

Without pausing from one motion to the next, Kreeg flexed his hind legs, lifted, and struck the earth with BlaKote's body.

To the Ur'Lugh, this must have been a shocking sight. One moment BlaKote was raised on the shoulders of the general, helpless with lack of breath, one arm clawing the empty air. The next moment he was down. Slammed into the ground on his side with mind-jarring impact.

BlaKote's jaw worked soundlessly. The spade of one shoulder twitched as he tried to scramble up and over, his left forepaw still reaching for some part of Kreeg—any part of Kreeg—on which he might inflict a scratch or a punch.

But it was too late. Kreeg didn't stop. Fights were won by seizing an advantage and bludgeoning or cutting or strangling one's enemies in their helplessness. He would not surrender the advantage, even to gloat. He kept BlaKote pinned, pressed his body into the ground, kept the shattered lungs from drawing breath by jamming one forelimb into the rat's throat.

He leaned forward and looked into BlaKote's unblinking eyes, saw the life swirling away.

He had been right.

Nothing.

For the benefit of the crew, he said, "Give my regards to GoRec."

For a moment, cold terror crept into his stomach. A chill spread through his body, expanding into a numb affirmation of nothingness, as hard and unfeeling as stone. Then he shook himself and rose from BlaKote's body. He drew himself to his full height, and, for effect, scraped the dirt from one finger in a gesture of nonchalance.

Self-confidence returned in a flood, rushing through him as he saw the expressions of admiration and fear.

He had not used War Claw. His old habits, his old skills, had not betrayed him. He had earned the title of master. He had doubled the size of his Crew. He had finalized the first phase in his plan to rid the universe, once and for all, of the mice of Tira-Nor.

WoKot stepped into the silence of the circle. He tipped his head at BlaKote's body. "Want me to haul off the leftovers?"

"No," Kreeg said. "Leave him."

26

JaRed

JaRed followed the moon. Its light slashed through the interwoven branches and fell on the forest floor like chips of blue ice. He kept to darkness, and though his legs ached, he stopped only to sniff the air for the scent of predators.

Before dawn he came across another mouse. It slept behind a mound of frozen leaves, its back lumped against a tree, head resting on one paw, its tail wrapped around its belly.

JaRed recognized him. He was a mouse of the kingsguard, a recently-promoted commoner.

The smell of other mice hung in the air. He must have stumbled across SoSheth and the full force of the kingsguard camped at the base of the stone wall.

He would have to walk through the camp in order to reach the crack in the wall.

A sense of buoyancy—a feeling of warmth and anger and indignation—flooded through him. Though his own good sense told him to back away and wait for SoSheth to leave, he found himself stepping forward.

He would walk through the camp. Here and now he would find out if ElShua was really with him.

He moved past the sleeping sentry and past a dense growth of trees sparkling with frost. A moment later he stood in the midst of a great encampment. A mass of sleeping mice, spread out like so many stones under the night sky, all of them asleep.

Odd. Not so much as a snore. Stillness lay over the camp like a shawl. The kingsguard never slept so quietly.

JaRed bathed in the strangeness of the moment. On the far side of the clearing, moonlight painted the limestone face of the wall. As he waited, power flowed through him, inexhaustible and terrifying.

Under his breath he said, "What must I do?"

Silence.

He turned and took in the sight of the bodies, thinking that they lay like the dead; not unlike the corpses in his recurring nightmares.

Then he noticed King SoSheth asleep under a dry leaf.

JaRed took a few steps in that direction, paused, then continued. He stood over SoSheth in the moonlight and stared down.

A flood of hatred rose in his chest. He couldn't stop

it, couldn't hold back the bitterness that brought a sour taste of bile to his throat. For a moment he wanted nothing in the world so much as to kill. He saw himself reach out with both paws and crush the king's windpipe.

SoSheth's body fell from the grip of the Badger and thudded next to him, the eyes wide and lifeless.

A voice, soft as new grass, slipped into JaRed's ears. "What is the worst thing that can happen to you?"

He stared.

The worst thing? The very worst thing? Not death. Death wasn't the worst thing that could happen.

I could become like him. That's the worst thing that could happen to me.

I could become like SoSheth.

He brushed back the shock of fur on his forehead and sighed. He stood there for what seemed a long time as the kingsguard dozed around him.

Near SoSheth's upturned face, frozen together on the frosted ground, lay a clump of raisins. A midnight snack for his highness.

JaRed picked up the raisins and tiptoed through the sleeping mice to the edge of the trees. He looked heavenward, wondering who stood sentry at the top of the Wall.

He strode through the emptiness to the crack, stuffed the raisins into his cheeks, and began to climb.

27

HaRed

Moonlight slanted into the washtub. It spilled through flaking rust-holes and pillared the darkness in bright beams, illuminating the smoky columns of HaRed's breath. The light hinted deliciously at warmth, but did not achieve it.

HaRed sat with his back propped against the galvanized wall of the washtub, one hand clasped across his thigh. The flow of blood had stopped, but his leg throbbed with pain. Loss of blood made him sleepy, in spite of the night air seeping into his bones.

A piece of the washtub must have broken off inside his leg. Worse, he now knew what the rats were planning. He knew what was about to happen to Tira-Nor.

After the duel, the rat leader sang out his instructions. His commands were loud and explicit, delivered in short, terse sentences with a convincing threat of dire consequences for failure.

Kreeg was intelligent as well as cruel, calculating, and driven by motives HaRed could not fathom. GoRec had terrified the mice of Tira-Nor with supernatural strength and speed. Kreeg terrified HaRed because he thought of everything.

How did the rat master know about Tira-Nor's wall stones, double-backs, and fool's errands? How had he learned the layout of the Great Hall, or the location of the inner gates separating the Families and Kingsguard from the Commons?

HaRed straightened his leg, wincing as splinters of pain stabbed his thigh. He could not get out the way he had come in.

A host of more immediate questions bombarded his mind. Would he be able to walk? And if so, how far? Would the wound reopen? Would loss of blood kill him before he reached the Wall? How would he climb once he got there?

But before he could walk, he must escape the prison of the washtub.

He shifted his weight, told himself the pain would lessen with time. He rose to one knee, the injured leg held out straight. His pulse pounded in his thigh. His stomach lurched.

He steadied himself, jammed his left forepaw against the washtub wall, and clawed the dirt at the base with his right.

TWENTY SEVEN

The ground, tufted here and there by dead grass, felt like pavement. Hard as stone.

He paused, contemplating the enormity of the danger he faced. No one knew where he was! Then he speared the ground with the claws of his right paw and began to scratch out a shallow hole.

In an hour he had barely dented the earth.

He kept digging. He would not consider the possibility of failure.

Tira-Nor must get word of Kreeg's plan. JaRed must be warned.

At last HaRed had found purpose. After a lifetime of searching for meaning, he discovered the secret at last. He knew why he had been born.

The mice of Tira-Nor needed him.

28

Kreeg

The mice standing sentry inside the East Gate died badly. This pleased Kreeg, who led the invasion himself, descending first into the empty darkness of the gate.

The closest sentry made the mistake of huddling inside the tunnel to keep warm, and died without seeing his attacker. The second sentry shouted the alarm, and then he too fell to War Claw.

Two other sentries emerged from the guard chamber to the side of the tunnel. One went down under WoKot's full weight and was ripped apart in a matter of seconds. The other bolted for the trip-lever that would seal off the city from the gate complex.

Kreeg hurled himself after the escaping mouse and caught its tail just as it leapt into the alcove. He heaved the mouse back into the tunnel and cracked its head against the wall.

The crew bubbled around him. "Nice goin', boss. He'll have a pretty headache in the mornin'. Har har har."

None of the Ur'Lugh took part in the opening skirmish. Only Kreeg's trusted scum, the long-timers. He had crafted other plans for BlaKote's former gang.

He found WoKot in the gate complex storeroom, beating an overeager rat for stealing a mouthful of sunflower seeds without permission.

"What's the boss say 'bout scroungin', Mangey?"

Mangey, paws caging his ears, stammered pitifully, "Mangey thought ... I thought that ... you know, Woksie, that we was to eat sumpin'. What with all the excitement. And you know how Mangey gets when I a'vent ad dinsies in two days."

"But you did know the orders, didn't you?"

"Weeellll," Mangey said. "Seems like maybe someone said sumpin' 'bout waiting for the okey-doke."

"And so?" WoKot stroked his chin.

"What do you mean, and so?"

He smiled with exaggerated pity, an expression that looked so out of place on his long, scarred face that Mangey's eyes widened. "And sooooo, what do you think your punishment should be, dear Mangey?"

Mangey's lower jaw worked like the handle of an unprimed pump. "I ... um ... er ..."

"Right. An eye or an ear is what the code calls for. Ain't that right, Mangey?" WoKot glimpsed Kreeg standing in the entry hole. "General?"

Kreeg expected something like this to happen. "I think Mangey would look very nice with less ear on the left side." There were a few laughs. Mangey was one of the less popular scumdevils. "However, since we are in a frightful hurry, and since my plan calls for precise obedience to all of my orders, and since Mangey has shown no inclination to such precision..." He thrust the tip of War Claw under Mangey's quivering chin. "I can't think of any good reason not to just have done with him."

Mangey whimpered.

WoKot peered over Mangey's shoulder, playing his part splendidly. "On the other paw, boss, we do need someone to watch this entrance. And Mangey here, being worthless in a fight, might make a decent sentry. He is, after all, pretty good at sitting around doing nothing."

This brought more laughter from the other rats.

Kreeg inspected the delicate sheen on War Claw. He had applied eleven coats of the dark liquid from the jar, and two mice were dead. War Claw still carried enough poison for a fair number of kills.

"All right," he said at last. "Mangey, I'm going to give you a second chance. Not because you deserve it, but because I think you might be useful. Understand that, Mangey? You will live as long as you are useful to me. And you are useful to me here. Guarding the food in this storeroom. When I come back, I'm going to find you here, aren't I, Mangey?"

Mangey nodded, his eyes wide.

"When I come back, you aren't going to have eaten any of this food. Are you, Mangey?"

He shook his head.

"When I come back, you are going to be here, and all the food is going to be here. Right, Mangey?"

He nodded.

Kreeg tickled the rat's chin with the point of War Claw, enjoying the hungry expression it produced on the faces of the others. "Most important, this gate is going to remain open. Open, Mangey. You're not going to let any mouse near that alcove. That's not so hard to understand, is it?"

He shook his head again.

"Good. Then it's time for the rest of us to get busy." Kreeg nodded to WoKot. "You have your orders."

29

Blang

Blang awoke in darkness. Greenish wisps of light from the Great Hall oozed into his sleeping chamber off the southern barracks tunnel.

He no longer slept in the kingsguard section of Tira-Nor when on duty. He slept in the barracks off the Great Hall. He lay now in the same room that once housed RuHoff the Seer, TaMir's mentor, when the Great Hall was used as a temple. That was before SoSheth came to power; details of the transformation of the Great Hall remained sketchy.

Blang's previous quarters had been given to Captain YaGo. Blang told himself—and several of the officers—that this didn't bother him. He couldn't direct the militia if he weren't with them. Getting messages to and from the Commons on a routine basis would have been far more hassle than changing quarters.

But something about the Cadridian bothered him.

For one thing, Blang knew so little about YaGo, so little about where he came from. How could SoSheth trust a total stranger—a foreigner—with the security of Tira-Nor?

But then, LaRish had been a foreigner too. For that matter, Blang himself wasn't native-born to Tira-Nor. He had come to the city as a young mouse and had been taken in by two childless, older mice of the Lesser Families.

But Blang served many seasons under LaRish before promotion. Why hadn't the king promoted someone like KoVeek?

The king doesn't trust us. His judgment has eroded. The king is mad!

A sound drifted into his chamber from the Great Hall. Distant shouts. Someone called his name.

He resisted the urge to meet the messenger in the hall. Tira-Nor's militia lacked discipline; the last thing they needed was to see their commander scurrying like a cockroach at the slightest disturbance. Whatever it was would have to be brought to him.

"Blang! Colonel Blang!" A runner, breathless and fear-stricken, stumbled into his chambers.

"Lower your voice before you panic the whole barracks. What is it?"

"Rats!" the runner said. "Rats in the Wind Gate. Rats in the East Gate complex. Rats to the north as well. There's panic and—"

Blang stood. Rats? Inside the Commons? He thought of KahEesha and the baby. "How many?"

"Don't know. Could be hundreds. Thousands even."

"Don't give me could-be. Tell me what you know."

"LimJik was at the Wind Gate with the sentries." The runner panted, "Rats came down the hole and started killing. DriNin told him to go for help and tried to spring the wall stone, but must not have made it. I was at the Tower Gate when another runner from East Gate said there were rats killing all along the perimeter."

"Have any wall stones been activated?"

The mouse gulped. "That's just it, sir. The rats are closing the holes themselves!"

Blang scowled. Why would the rats close off the gate holes? Why would they lock themselves in? It didn't make sense.

Unless they knew the kingsguard was out of the city.

Panic rose in Blang's chest.

Lord Wroth, coming at last.

KahEesha!

Blang forced all emotion from his face. "Can you still run?"

The runner wiped his brow. "Yes, sir."

"Good. Run to the Kingsguard. If the sentries try to stop you, give them my name and use the word tunnelstorm. Tell Lieutenant HarViq to seal off the Families and Kingsguard. Tell him to notify King SoSheth at once."

"Yes, sir."

"Repeat it."

The mouse did, his eyes wide, terrified.

"And the code word?"

"Yes, sir. Thunder ... tunnelstorm."

Blang took a deep breath. He could not afford fear now. "After you deliver the message I will need you again."

"Yes, sir."

"And the code word?"

"Tunnelstorm. Sir."

"What's your name, son?"

"MeerQo."

"Very well, MeerQo. Get going." Blang paused for just a moment. Then, heart thumping against his ribs, he stepped into the main barracks. He spat orders at Lieutenant HarVik, ordering two quick response squads to the East Gate. He doubted he could resist the rats in two places. Better to win one skirmish and concede the other than to lose both. He would have to seal off the damage. He would have to gamble for more time.

He snapped his second set of instructions at Lieutenant Ryn. "I need three volunteers. Scouts. I need information, lieutenant. Where the rats are, how many we're up against, and what kind of damage they've done. I want to know if this is a lucky band of raiders, or an organized assault."

Ryn snapped a crisp salute and retreated, hand-picking the volunteers with the forefinger of his right paw.

Blang's third priority took precious seconds to execute. The available militia assembled in the Great Hall. They stood in a semicircle, their shoulders crammed together, every eye straining forward. Their hope rested with him, and he knew it. He prayed it was not misplaced.

"Give me four rows," he barked. The mice looked at each other, as though waiting for someone to move, and Blang was forced to raise his voice. "Four rows! Now!" There came a sudden flurry of movement, shifting, jostling elbows, and eyes looking around.

The lack of discipline flustered him. These weren't soldiers. Not yet. Perhaps one day the militia of Tira-Nor might be molded into a formidable force. But not now, not today. Today these mice were no more than scavengers who had drawn a short straw.

"Good," he said, though it was an obvious lie. "We haven't much time. Platoon One, you're going to seal off the northern quadrant east of the Great Hall. Platoon Two, you'll take the southern quadrant under Lieutenant Ryn. Platoon Three ... Where is Lieutenant Stenner?"

"Haven't seen him since last night," someone said.

Blang shook his head. "Corporal HoffMin?"

"Sir?" A young mouse with wide, darting eyes and stooped shoulders stepped forward.

"Take Platoon Three east of the Great Hall and hold the main corridor. Platoon Four will stay here in the Great Hall with me."

But Corporal HoffMin didn't move. "Colonel?" he asked.

"Yes?" Blang felt the last remnant of his patience peeling away.

"We're going to split the Commons in half?"

"If there is time, yes."

"But, sir ..."

Blang saw the looks on the faces of the mice and understood what they were thinking. The same fear tormented him.

KahEesha.

Blang looked HoffMin in the eye. "We're going to seal off east from west, corporal."

"Abandon those in the east?"

"We're going to save those in the west. If there's time."

From the far eastern corner, where the main corridor emptied into an antechamber off the Great Hall, came the distant echoes of screams.

Before the militia could exit the barracks, a great mass of terrified commoners pushed its way into the

Great Hall.

It was a mad scramble, a chaotic flood of terror-stricken stupidity. Grown mice shoved helpless kits aside, trampled the aged and infirm. Blind to everything but their fear.

Blang understood the cunning of the rat leader, whoever he was. The tunnels of the Commons would be so clogged with fleeing mice—mice rushing toward the western half of the commons—that the militia would be incapable of responding with a counterattack.

He remembered what MeerQo said about rats tripping the wall stones, sealing off the gate holes.

He knew what would happen. And there was nothing he could do to stop it.

30

SoSheth

SoSheth awakened slowly. His toes were numb, his back knotted by the cold earth. And these were not the only irritations.

A sound assaulted his ears. A voice like the coming of doom sliced the silence of the night, cut through the fog of his sleep, jolting him to awareness.

He blinked. Moonlight flooded the open glade, pouring through holes in the sky.

The voice irritated him even before he realized whose it was, before he knew the meaning of it.

"My ... lord ... and ... king!"

Mice stirred around him. The kingsguard roused itself at the thumping of the words. They rose to their elbows, shook their heads, looked around. Eyebrows raised all around the clearing.

"My ... lord ... and ... king!"

Louder now. Much louder. Punctuated by emo-

189

tion.

SoSheth rose and stalked through the glade, toward the sound of the voice. Moonlight slashed the darkness in vivid streaks, slanting through trees, bathing the slope of the massive Wall beyond the edge of the Dark Forest. Its stony face glowed in the darkness.

"King SoSheth!" The voice echoed above him, midway up the jagged scar of the crack in the Wall's surface.

SoSheth stepped from the edge of the trees. "JaRed?" Guilt crept into the coldness of his heart. He barely noticed as YaGo emerged next to him. "JaRed? Is that you?"

"Why are you hunting me?"

His body ached. His heart ached. *What have I been doing?* "JaRed?" SoSheth shouted through cupped paws. "Come down!"

The reply fell from the Wall. "Captain YaGo, you have failed. Why did you allow a thief to approach the king as he slept?"

YaGo hissed indignantly.

SoSheth snapped his head around to glare at YaGo, and saw rows of faces staring back at him. The entire force of the kingsguard was watching.

"Thief?" YaGo said. "I don't know what—"

The voice howled down. "Where, Captain YaGo? Where are the king's raisins?"

As if in answer they came, falling from the sky in rapid succession.

Lieutenant FaLin plodded forward, plucked one of the black shapes from the earth. He sniffed it, held it aloft as though to give it back to the king. "Raisin." When SoSheth didn't take it, he let it fall from his grip. "Highness."

SoSheth stared at the Wall. The runt had crept into their camp, had stolen the raisins while they all slept.

He could have killed me. Why didn't he?

Passion rose in his throat, but no words would come. *I have misjudged him. I should end this now. Bring him back. Grant him my pardon.*

But when he saw the faces of the kingsguard, the old hatred returned, roiling up with a new ferocity that came with the full force of understanding.

Slowly, like day changing to night, King SoSheth's mood changed.

The kingsguard resented him. Despised him. Hated him. He saw it in their eyes. Why had JaRed snuck into camp like a scurrying spider? Why had the little runt risked his life? SoSheth knew. JaRed had stolen more than raisins.

He had stolen the loyalty of the kingsguard.

SoSheth's eyes narrowed. "What are you looking at?"

Every eye turned away, but the unspoken accusations remained. *JaRed could have killed you, but didn't.*

You humiliated Blang. You killed TaMir. Now you're dragging us out here to murder JaRed.

Worst of all, the rumor that had drifted through the tunnels of Tira-Nor for weeks. *The King is mad!*

SoSheth ground his teeth together. *My only mistake was not killing the little waste-of-air when I had the chance.*

But there was no hope of capturing JaRed son of ReDemec while he remained atop the Wall. Which meant either a lengthy siege or a long, depressing march back to Tira-Nor.

He returned to his pallet and lay fuming as the kingsguard settled back to sleep around him, their silence an affront to his dignity.

When a messenger from Tira-Nor found him in the freezing gray fog of dawn, SoSheth still lay wide awake.

"My lord," the mouse said, chest heaving. "Tira-Nor is under attack. Colonel Blang begs your immediate return."

"Attack? What kind of attack?"

"Rats, majesty."

SoSheth kicked at a small stone and cursed under his breath. Now he had no choice. He must return to Tira-Nor. He would have to deal with the runt some other time. "Rouse the officers."

"If I may be so bold, my lawd," YaGo said, "returning to Tira-Nor now seems most unwise."

"There's more," the messenger continued. "On the way here I came across one of your southern patrols. The bridge those rats have been using is gone."

"How?"

The messenger shook his head. "Don't know. But if you come back now the rats will have nowhere to hide. You can pin them against the cliffs of the White River."

Captain YaGo shoved the messenger aside with one arm and bowed elegantly. "Foolishness, my Lawd."

"But Your Majesty—"

SoSheth held up one paw for silence, then motioned to YaGo. "Make your point."

"It is a trap."

He rubbed his temples. A trap? Confusion pricked a throbbing ache behind his forehead. "What do you mean?"

"You have not consulted your God."

"I don't have a God, captain."

YaGo shrugged. "We know rats have schemed to raid our supply rooms. What better place to plan an ambush than at the edge ahv the forest?"

SoSheth looked up. Fog blotted the tops of the trees. Sunlight, concealed by a white curtain, accented the frosted sticks of the trees. He felt as though his body heat were being sucked away by something cold and dead, a leech on his soul. "And there is still the runt," he said.

"Yes, my lawd."

SoSheth turned, scratched the side of his face with one paw. Nervousness tugged at him, though he did not know why.

I don't have a God.

He missed Captain Blang suddenly, missed the unspoken familiarity. He hardly knew YaGo.

He cleared his throat. "What God do you serve, YaGo? What do they teach young mice in Cadrid about such things?"

YaGo spoke carefully. "In the legends we are told that Lord Wroth transformed the ancients into rats through some dark magick known only to him. Ahv course, such magick is forbidden by ElShua. And yet. It is curious ..."

"What is curious?"

"Well. The black magick in the story worked. The old legends of ElShua only prove that there is another kind ahv power, a power that can be used. ElShua forbids it. But He doesn't say why."

"In the story," SoSheth said, thinking back, "the rats are cursed by an insatiable appetite for garbage."

YaGo smiled. "Is that worse than dried seeds and withering berries?"

"What about you, captain?"

"I am a servant ahv Kalla."

SoSheth felt a momentary thrill, a jolt like the slow-motion terror of falling in a dream. TaMir had spoken the name Kalla before he died. "What are you suggesting, captain?"

YaGo bobbed his head. "The medium ahv Kalla. A sort ahv ... spell. Based on a legend told in Cadrid for generations. They say a rat lived among us, under the protection ahv my great-great grandfather, the Lord Regent. This rat—who was ancient even when she first appeared—was adept in the arts ahv the priests ahv Wroth. She was a great sorceress who wove astounding riddles, distilled potions from the raw vapors ahv the night, and drew dead spirits from the heart ahv the earth."

SoSheth raised one eyebrow, surprised to hear such talk coming from the mouth of his second-in-command. "Her name, I suppose, was Kalla?"

YaGo bowed. "Lieutentant ThuBrik, who accompanied me to Tira-Nor from Cadrid, served as acolyte at the temple ahv Wroth for many years. He received training in the mystery arts, and assures me he has mastered a number ahv the more difficult incantations. One ahv which is called after the Dame Kalla's penchant for communicating with departed spirits."

For weeks the world seemed to have been capsizing. First GoRec, then JaRed, then TaMir and Blang, then the fresh attacks on Tira-Nor. And now, priests of Wroth had risen among SoSheth's kingsguard, and without his knowledge. He didn't know whether to be irritated or pleased. He cleared his throat. "How would communicating with the dead help me today, captain? Since my goal is to avoid joining them."

"To be blunt, My Lawd, the acolytes ahv Wroth have never been good at fortune-telling. Perhaps that is why their magic is called a mystery art. The future is an area in which, I'm afraid, only the Seers have any claim to accuracy ahv vision. Therefore, My Lawd, you must converse with TaMir once again. His spirit will be far more powerful in death than in life."

SoSheth stared. Ask TaMir? Talk to a ghost? The idea terrified and thrilled him. TaMir had always warned against dabbling with sorcery, spells, and departed spirits. And yet ... "How long does it take?" he asked. "What must be done?"

YaGo whistled, and Lieutenant ThuBrik lurched toward them through the brightening gray wash of morning.

"My Lawd." Lips drawn back in a perpetual sneer, ThuBrik bowed.

"Captain YaGo has been telling me about the Medium of Kalla."

A slow, nervous smile stretched across ThuBrik's snout. "A most interesting spell. Most interesting."

"How is it done?"

Thubrik's brow arched above bloodshot eyes. "I must be given the ingredients." He counted off items against the digits of one paw. "A shallow pit, various herbs, the spirit's genealogical name, the incantation, which, happily, I have committed to memory, and, ahv course, an offering."

SoSheth blinked. "An offering?"

"A sacrifice. A life. Or, to be more precise, a death."

YaGo waved one hand dismissively. "A criminal would do, correct?"

ThuBrik tilted his head. "Innocence is not valued in the mystery arts, captain. Though ahv course the loss ahv innocence is. In this case, it will not matter if the blood is black, as they say."

YaGo turned to the king. "Consider the lives that will be spared by the sacrifice ahv one mouse. You will be allowed to see into the future. TaMir will show you exactly what to do. You will be saving lives."

"By killing?"

"Death, my lawd! Death is the most powerful magic there is. And fortunately, we happen to have a mouse under arrest for treason."

"Who?"

"HoVich. The sentry who allowed the runt into camp this morning."

SoSheth clenched his jaw into a tight knot of hatred. "Runt."

"Yes."

"HoVich let him into my camp. Let him steal my raisins. Let him steal the loyalty of my kingsguard."

"Yes, my lawd."

SoSheth's gaze flicked from YaGo to ThuBrik. "How soon can it be done?"

"But Your Highness." The messenger needled in from the shadows, his head swiveling stupidly from face to face. "What about the quarry rats? What about the opportunity of the fallen bridge? What about Tira-Nor, Your Highness?"

SoSheth ignored the interruption. "Lieutenant ThuBrik, I asked you a question. How soon can the Medium of Kalla be done?"

ThuBrik smiled. "Within the hour."

31
JaRed

JaRed climbed the rest of the way in silence. After the racket he had made, any sentry at the top of the wall had to be awake.

He cast a final look down. Far below him, the kingsguard melted back into the shadows of the trees.

"Astonishing," a familiar voice said. "I wouldn't have believed it if I didn't see it with my own eyes."

A paw helped him to the top.

Colonel Gibbs beamed at him. "And that business on the lake, when the rascals were almost on top of you, snapping at your very heels. Using your size to such—dare I say it?—weighty advantage. Brilliant!"

"The lake? How do you know about that?"

"Saw it, of course. You can see the lake from here. At least, you can see it in daylight." Gibbs pointed. To the west, beyond the sheer drop of the wall, the black canopy of the Dark Forest lay shrouded in fog.

Here and there, jagged fingers broke through the moonstruck haze, some still cloaked in dead leaves. In the distance the trees opened around a swath of polished white.

Behind Gibbs, Dimble and a dozen grenadiers approached.

"But what are you doing here?" JaRed asked.

Gibbs clapped JaRed across the back. "Seems you were right about King SoSheth. Wasn't interested in our help. He actually gave us the heave-ho! Can you believe that?"

"Yes."

"The outlanders have agreed to let us stay with them." He gestured east, past Dimble and the half-circle of grenadiers.

A lonely, one-room chapel jutted from the crown of the hill. It was small for a manmade structure. Squatting on a base of cut stones, most of its windows were hung with sheets of weathered plywood. Chipped paint freckled its white spire in the moonlight.

"They needed someone to guard the way up, and we needed a temporary base of operations. So here we are."

"I thought you didn't like the outlanders."

"Never said that. Just said I didn't think you'd be happy with them. Haven't changed my mind, either." Gibbs took JaRed's elbow and led him toward the chapel. As he did, Dimble gave the order for the grenadiers to fall out. Soon a dozen mice were congratulating him with handshakes, back-slaps, and tail-twists.

"Well done, JaRed!"

"The cunnel was right about you. Said you were sent."

"Good to 'ave you back!"

Dimble finally shooed the smiling grenadiers away, and Gibbs walked with JaRed to the far side of the building. "I have alerted the one called Bigums. He is expecting you. He will, I think, be glad that you survived. But don't expect a great deal of gratitude."

Inside, mildew, candle wax, and ancient wood polish mingled with the stale odors of wet grain and sickness.

Piles of shredded cardboard lay heaped onto the carpeted floor of the chapel. The moon threw dull strings of color through the stained glass over the altar, staining the long wooden pews red and blue.

Faces peered at him from under the pews. The outlanders, the grenadiers, the women and children of the north meadows. Scavengers and foreign fighters and refugees with gaunt bodies.

A hollow-cheeked female with enormous black eyes risked a smile and then retreated into the shadows.

Bigums, reclining with his back to the altar, held

aloft what appeared to be a blackening chunk of an ear of corn. "Outlanders of the north meadows. This is your kernel speaking!" He laughed. A few of the others joined him, but the effect did not last, and the fat mouse did not let the ensuing silence linger. "Ha! Ha ha ha!" He waved the corn in the air for emphasis. "Kernel. Not king. We have no kings here, have we?" He motioned for JaRed to approach. "Come, come, Ratbane. You too, Colonel Gibbs. I see you made it to our winter fortress. I am most pleased. But you will have to pull your weight. We are all equals here. We don't allow freeloaders."

"Of course not," JaRed said.

"And I daresay you've done enough for one evening. But the colonel. Well. There's another matter entirely."

Gibbs raised one eyebrow. "We have an agreement."

"Indeed we do. You promised us protection and entertainment for as long as you're here."

"I did," Gibbs said.

"Well, then. Entertain us!"

Gibbs bowed, his dignity apparently unruffled.

"'Ow about a story, colonel?" a grenadier said.

"If you please, colonel?"

"The one about the badger?"

Gibbs turned a slow circle. "Again?"

Mouse kits edged closer, their eyes eager.

"Yes, I suppose I could do that one."

"Go on, then, colonel!" A grenadier clapped his paws. "Give us a ripper!"

In front of the altar, Bigums took a huge bite from the chunk of corn in his hand. "That's right. A ripper! And don't be quick about it. We have all night."

JaRed glanced around the room. The sour, undying smells. The bodies jammed into darkness. The sense of being cut off from the rest of the world. Something about this place bothered him, made him think of a shell with no nut.

"Long ago," Gibbs said, "before the Great Owl made his first visit to our skies. Before Lord Wroth haunted the realm between heaven and earth ..."

No hope. JaRed settled on the carpet to listen. *Nothing to live for. Nothing to die for.*

In the background, Gibbs's voice painted the shadows. "Before ElShua first planted the seed of our world in the soil of His great garden, a terrible war raged in the heavens ..."

That's why the outlanders laugh. To help them forget they're not living.

As Gibbs talked on, JaRed realized what he had forgotten. He pulled himself to all fours. "Bigums?"

Gibbs stopped speaking.

The fat outlander grunted. He sat with his eyes half shut. With one paw he motioned for JaRed to be quiet.

JaRed ignored the gesture. "Bigums, where is my brother? Where is HaRed?"

One eyelid fluttered open. Underneath, the eye rolled in its socket and found JaRed's face. Accusingly unhappy. "Dunno."

"Did he come up the Wall?"

Scrounger answered. "Haint seen him. He didn't make it up the Wall."

"Did you see him below the Wall?" JaRed glanced around the room. The mouse kits gathered around Gibbs rubbed their eyes. "Did any of you?"

No one answered.

JaRed clenched his fists. "At least have the decency to say something."

Bigums pulled himself erect. "Joke anyone?"

From the back of the room a female whispered, "He isn't here, Ratbane."

Bigums coughed a great hacking cough and spat into the mound of shredded newspaper at his feet. "Remember our motto. It's how we survive. Every mouse for himself."

"Or herself," someone said.

"Right. Or herself. We don't talk about those who lag behind. It spoils the fun."

Gibbs flicked a knowing look at JaRed and shook his head.

"It's late," Bigums said. "Too late for the colonel's story. Call it even. All debts for the day are paid."

JaRed stepped toward Bigums. "Did HaRed make it to the wall?"

Bigums sighed. "We don't know where Glumface has gone to, but he's probably fine. Probably frowning somewhere down among the trees. He'll turn up. In the meantime, why don't you leave these poor devils alone? Let us get some sleep?" He turned his back to JaRed, shook his belly, and stretched out on one side.

JaRed clenched his teeth. The feeling of emptiness he had struggled with earlier returned in full force, nearly knocking him to his knees. He stared at Bigums' back, trying to understand the thoughts spinning together in his mind.

Something the fat outlander said gnawed at him.

"Why don't you leave these poor devils alone?"

Gibbs stepped over protesting kits and reached for JaRed's arm. "Come on. The grenadiers can help. I've been sending patrols down the Wall. Maybe one of my scouts can tell us something."

Suddenly the answer came to him. The explanation. The feeling of hopelessness, of having been here before.

These poor devils.

He knew who the outlanders reminded him of. He cast one final glance over his shoulder and stepped into the pre-morning chill.

32

HaRed

The earth resisted the bony shovels of HaRed's paws. His fingers were cracked and stiff as twigs. His paws bled from the slices on both palms, throbbing in rhythm with the pounding pain in his thigh.

All day he attacked the ground, scraping back dirt from the rounded rim where the washtub met the earth, scooping out tiny clod after tiny clod, until the dimple became a bowl, and the bowl became a crevice, and the crevice edged under the wall to freedom.

A stubborn resolve cemented his heart and made the pain endurable. Even when the ache in his head ignited a slow burn.

Night fell. During the day he shivered in the cold and gloom of the prison. As the sun set, the brilliant shafts of fire spiking through the roof faded away to blackness, but HaRed grew hotter. Fever gripped him, smoldering in his face, his neck, his limbs. Sweat coated the skin beneath his fur, dripped and splashed onto the cold turf in little rivers.

Still, he dug.

He lay half in and half out of the makeshift tunnel, stiff as a wet sheet under snow, folded like a piece of wire.

Sometime during the night, when the moon hung low on the horizon and lay all but hidden behind an umbrella of leafless limbs, he slipped into the freedom of the night air.

A rat faced him from the far side of the clearing, its body pressed low to the ground. Kreeg had left a sentry.

Well, then, let it come. Let it kill me quickly.

The rat didn't move. HaRed sucked in cold gulps of air and blinked at the stars, hope kindling in his chest again. Perhaps the rat slept. It hadn't moved so much as a hair. Its tail, which should have coiled and flicked in anticipation, remained motionless.

The truth dawned on him.

The Ur'Lugh didn't honor each other in life, why would they do so in death?

It was BlaKote. And he was dead.

HaRed braced himself, feeling suddenly cold. His sweat-dampened fur clung to his skin in patches, and the night breeze brought a shiver to his spine. His limbs shook. His leg was dead weight, a log split down the middle, seared by a pain that would not relent.

Daylight stood far off. He would have to make his way north and west through the Dark Forest to the Wall by moonlight. He would have to navigate by dumb luck. And if he could not climb the Wall when he got there, then, well, JaRed would take care of him.

If JaRed had survived SoSheth. And Kreeg.

Fear crept into HaRed's belly. The dead weight of his legs grew. A stiffness that made movement clumsy.

Fear hammered at the back door of his brain. He could not make the return journey to the Wall. He could not make the shorter trip to Tira-Nor to beg for mercy. He lacked the strength. He would die somewhere in the Black Unknown, lost and alone forever.

No.

He stood, his good leg shaking with fatigue, his bad leg protesting violently. He shuffled forward, resisting the pain, and limped past BlaKote's body. He did not look at it, but headed into the trees toward the Wall.

Hour after hour dragged by. He did not know how long or how far he walked. The moon disappeared behind a gray veil. His body grew numb.

He was made of wood. The cold skin of the earth gripped his soul, frosting over the desire to live, to move, to breathe. His body froze into a solid lump, outside in, like the surface of a pond. At some point his skin would shatter into thousands of brittle pieces.

Just before dawn he stumbled and fell.

The wound came alive. Pain sliced upward along his thigh, drove a red-hot spike through the muscle into bone.

He grasped his leg in both hands, felt warmth there, real warmth, pulsing, pouring out. His lifeblood spilled into a dark pool of shadow and glistened as it froze.

JaRed would come for him.

Laughter rang in his mind. *JaRed? JaRed will come for you! JaRed doesn't know mousey's here!*

He stared heavenward. In the east, night had already begun its daily retreat, yielding to purple the color of an old bruise where the mightiest trees of the forest fanned the sky.

There would be no last-minute rescue party. No one knew where he was. The result of his own cleverness, his own stupid heroics. He had left in secret, so only his own life would be risked. He had not thought such gambles were sometimes lost. Death always happened to someone else.

He watched the stars winking out one by one as numbness crept upward through his ankles. What he needed was sleep. Just a little. Just a moment. He would close his eyes and then open them in a minute.

No. I must warn JaRed. I must warn Tira-Nor.

But he could not move, could not stand, could not even turn over onto his stomach.

He spent his whole life wanting to do something important, something grand. Instead, he brought shame to his own family, and catastrophe to his brother. And at the end, just when he found an opportunity to make amends ...

"I've wasted my whole life."

Above, the stars dimmed to shards of broken glass.

He spoke again, needing to hear the sound of someone's voice. "I finally tried to do something for others, and it turns out not to have mattered. It won't make any difference. No one even knows."

Loneliness settled over him. Thankfully, the numbness reached his legs, and the pain—at last— began to fade away beyond reach, if not beyond memory.

"Stupid. I've been so stupid."

Something thudded behind him. A sound like a great weight falling to earth. He did not trust his ears, and he could not turn his head to look. And anyway, what did it matter now? The world was fading, washing to a dull gray.

He felt another vibration in the ground, and another, like massive footsteps.

A badger towered over him, blotting the trees, the early morning sky. "Stupid?" Its voice rumbled. "You have not been stupid, HaRed son of ReDemec. Only small."

HaRed blinked. *Small?* Yes, he was small. He had been small his whole life, but had never admitted it, even to himself. Especially to himself. He raised one paw, as though to ward off danger, but the Badger only stooped and nudged his body with its long snout.

"Are you going to kill me?"

A great sigh. A warm, gentle breath on his face. "No."

HaRed's tongue moved. He could not feel it, but he heard his own voice clearly. "Please. Warn JaRed."

"That task was given to you."

"It's too late." His mouth felt as dry as paper.

"It isn't."

"Why are you here?"

The Badger looked up.

HaRed saw, like sunlight glinting on ice, a crescent of white spiraling down from a rip in the sky.

"Because ... I did not want you to be alone."

HaRed let out a long, slow breath and closed his eyes.

33

SoSheth

The fog should have burned away by now.

Instead, it thickened into a white shroud, wrapped itself around the hulking trees, choked the air, and settled motionless over the dead body.

SoSheth drew a sharp breath. In truth, he had not believed in such rites. But something was, indeed, happening. The air grew colder. It hissed from his lungs in painful curls that mingled with the dense fog.

The fur at the base of his neck stood on end.

Even YaGo seemed to sense it, kneeling there with shoulders hunched, his head bowed.

YaGo. Who carried unpleasant, and yet useful, secrets.

The dimple in the earth moved. The shallow hole. The earthen bowl into which the vile substance of ThuBrik's spell had been dribbled, hardening as it froze. It shimmered, hissed, and rotated like a wheel. Black smoke jetted from its surface, which popped and crackled as bubbles globbed to the surface. Above it, the smoke expanded, became a pillar that rose skyward, writhing and churning in a circular dance mimicking the slow movement of the bowl. In the pillar a face appeared. The face of a rat. SoSheth recognized it, though he dare not say the name. He had seen a statue of it once before.

Lord Wroth.

Except now the face changed. The long needle nose receded. The teeth turned inward. The smoke above changed from black to gray, and from gray to white.

A sound like a door creaking on rusty hinges escaped the center of the pillar.

"Why have you disturbed meeeeeee?"

SoSheth froze where he sat. He could not move, though indeed the earth seemed to be moving around him.

YaGo bowed, face down. Lieutenant ThuBrik smiled, his bulbous eyes wide and eager.

"TaMir?" SoSheth asked.

But the voice was not TaMir's. Devoid of kindness, this voice spat like grease hitting a fire. "What do you want?"

SoSheth panicked. He stared up into the gloomy white smoke of the old Seer's face and could not remember what he wanted to ask. He clutched at his throat, could not breathe, felt as though his limbs were long chunks of ice.

Slowly, the pillar of smoke stopped revolving. The face in the smoke expanded, pressed outward, filling the space between them until the long misty nose pressed to the tip of SoSheth's own. The terrible vacant smoke-eyes widened, staring through him into his soul.

A hand took shape from the chest of the column, drawing after it a long, waspish arm. Smoke claws raked at SoSheth's cheek. Smoke fingers squeezed around his throat.

"Tell me," SoSheth blurted, finding his voice at last, "tell me what I must do!"

But the face was changing again. Long teeth jutted from the choking pattern of the face, and the eyes became black as wells.

"Dooo?" The voice crackled like a log popping into flame. "Go back, you fool! Back to Tira-Nor! Go back ... and DIE!"

SoSheth scrambled backward. He kicked at the earth and tried to turn, but the gray-black smoke of the pillar's hand held him. A pile of dead leaves and loose dirt, mounded from the bowl, erupted in a small shower as SoSheth struggled. Clogs of earth hit the blood in the bowl and hissed there.

The face in the pillar dimpled. Pocks appeared,

wide sores like boils that marred the smoky column and began to spread. The black eyes rolled back, widened, disappeared altogether.

"No!" ThuBrik said. "No, don't go!"

SoSheth fell, thumping into the ground with a jolt. He stumbled away, toward the main body of the kingsguard, his stomach churning with nausea even as he lurched through the trees. All around him voices screamed, the sound of sergeants giving orders. A great thrumming like thunder shook the trees where he had left the main body of his kingsguard warriors.

He ran forward, toward the sounds of confusion.

The sounds of battle.

He stumbled over something, his rear paw catching on a lump of fur. He caught himself, turned to rise, and saw the face of Corporal GinNiss staring back at him. Eyes open, unseeing.

He stood and ran on. His breath came in heaves, and despite the cold air, he was sweating; beads of perspiration ran beneath the long gray of his fur, chilling him.

A battle raged nearby. He saw another corpse, and another.

He pushed through a maze of dark shapes. Mice fled toward him. They didn't see him, didn't stop to salute, didn't return his shouted commands, nor answer his frantic, repeated question, "What's happening?"

At last he emerged into the center of the camp and saw, rising up, a black and silver shape that towered over him as a bear towers over a cat.

It turned, teeth bared, its eyes white. Around it, the fog that ghosted everything parted. Starlight fell from its black coat, beads of light that scattered through the patchwork shadows of the forest.

A badger.

Its hind legs stood not on the earth, but in the earth. It waded through the soil of the forest floor as a man might wade through water. And still it towered over him.

Then its eyes found him, and he forgot the terror of the smoke pillar. His legs gave way. He was powerless to resist, powerless to run, powerless to fight.

From the throat of the badger a low growl issued, and for a moment its eyes narrowed. Then it turned, strode past him, and was gone.

When he could move again, SoSheth ran.

Toward home.

Toward Tira-Nor.

34

JaRed

Below him, fog still blanketed the Dark Forest. Here on the stony ridge of the Wall it had all but burned away as the sun climbed. JaRed stared down at the black limbs swimming in the cloudy surface below. There would be kingsguard mice standing sentry, watching for signs of movement. He hoped these taut Grenadiers were as good at fighting as they were drilling. Even if they were, they would need the cover of the fog to escape notice.

JaRed led the way.

It was like drowning in a cloud. One moment he was looking out of the shadows of the crack at the silvery skin of the fog, the reflected sunlight almost painful to look at, and the next moment the world lay blanketed in a vast gray cloak. He saw nothing beyond the vertical edges of the crack, nothing but mist. No breeze stirred the air, and a heavy silence hung over everything, as though the forest were ashamed.

JaRed lowered himself to the grass at the base of the Wall and waited until Dimble dropped to his side. · He pointed to the left, indicating the direction they were to go, and then moved, pressing himself against the stones. Gibbs would follow with Dimble and the first of the Grenadiers.

He slipped across the open space, his eyes and ears alert for anything. Nothing stirred. Even as he approached the closest of the trees and saw its black chest looming out of gray shadow, he knew something was wrong.

He crept into the darker, more sinister fog under the trees. By now he should have seen or heard something. Surely King SoSheth posted sentries on his perimeter?

Or had the king finally come to his senses?

With the bridge destroyed, Kreeg was effectively trapped. SoSheth must have moved the kingsguard to deal with the rat general.

JaRed breathed a sigh of relief. He had not been confident the king would do the right thing, the sensible thing, the kingly thing.

But then, if King SoSheth had moved the kingsguard to attack Kreeg, why the odd silence, the death-like gloom?

Just as he was about to turn back, he saw the body.

A kingsguard mouse, prostrate by a great tree.

THIRTY FOUR

Blood roped from a wound in its throat to a shallow basin scraped from the earth.

JaRed edged closer. He recognized the contorted face. It was HoVich.

Tracks of mice ran in chaotic loops around the clearing. JaRed could tell nothing from them. He moved deeper into the woods. Soon he saw a second body, this one raked by giant claws. Then another. Corporal ErWin, lying at the base of a tree, his neck broken, but wearing an expression of surprising serenity.

It seemed half the kingsguard lay dead.

A gasp, startling in the silence, caught his attention. He stole closer to the source of the sound.

HaRed lay motionless on his side, one leg covered in blood. When he caught sight of JaRed, he flailed the air weakly with one arm.

JaRed stumbled to his side, pressed a palm to HaRed's face. "HaRed, it's me. What happened?" He looked down at his brother's leg. Bile rose in his throat. Not even RuHoff the Wise could heal such a wound.

HaRed's eyes focused. "JaRed?"

"Yes."

His lower jaw quivered as he raised his head. "Kreeg is after Tira-Nor."

"I know. Don't worry, SoSheth will stop him. The storerooms are safe."

"No, brother. Listen. Kreeg isn't after the store-rooms. He's after the whole city. He's going to ... seal off the gates ... kill everyone."

"How do you know this?"

"Overheard him."

"But what about SoSheth? Didn't he cut Kreeg off? Where is the kingsguard? Where is the king?"

But JaRed needed no answer. For suddenly he understood. The mice of Tira-Nor had been duped. They had run blindly into a trap that would destroy them all.

Kreeg had used him as bait to draw SoSheth away from Tira-Nor. And now the kingsguard lay dead in the Dark Forest, and the city had no hope.

Because of me.

"The king," HaRed said, "is right here."

JaRed squeezed HaRed's paws. *This is all my fault. I led SoSheth away from the city. I should have seen this. I should have led the king back to Tira-Nor. TaMir was wrong about me. He was wrong about ElShua.*

ElShua is a lie.

JaRed began to weep. He tried to stop himself, and failed. His shoulders shook as though with chill.

HaRed's head fell back to the forest floor. His eyes took on a distant look. His voice came as a whisper. "Forgive ..." His lungs emptied in a long, almost inaudible sigh, "us ..."

35

DeStra

Desperate screams. Shrieks. Curses in the passage. DeStra WilloWind had never heard so much noise in the tunnels of the Great Families.

Too frightened to move, she paused in the passage. Should she try to make it back to the YuLooq mansion? Or should she look for KahEesha?

Her father had warned her against crossing over into the Commons, but she didn't listen. After two weeks of visits, she considered KahEesha her friend. And now that Kah's kit, Norrie, was finally born, she spent more time in the ReDemec home than in her own.

Mice appeared in the distance, shoved along by an irresistible wall of pressing bodies, a cacophony of noises tumbling after them.

"Rats!"

"Attacking the Commons ..."

"Wall stones tripped too late."

"Killing."

"Must let us in."

"Pity!"

"Lord Wroth himself ..."

Grim-faced mice pushed past her. Throat dry, she made up her mind and began to walk again, intent on reaching the Lesser Families. She shoved her way through an increasing current of panicked mice crashing through the hallway and spilling in smaller waves into the alcoves and quarters on either wall.

A plan formed in DeStra's mind. She ducked into a side passage and sprinted east, then raced up the sloping tunnel leading to the Open Gate complex. Instead of climbing the tunnel that led to the gate hole, she ran down the main east-west tunnel, one of only two passages connecting the Commons with the Families.

What if Kah has already left?

But no. Not with a newborn. KahEesha wasn't a mouse to panic.

The flow of mice lessened. Most of the mice were coming from the kingsguard section, which stood at the highest level of the city. DeStra squeezed herself against the tide of fleeing mice, then pressed into an alcove on the north side of the hall.

She knew the alcove well. It lay on the west side of the guard-chamber that shielded those with power from those with nothing. As a child, she used to hide there during games.

She poked her head around the corner. In the distance, gray lumps fled toward the Great Hall as chamber after chamber emptied and the mice of the Commons abandoned their homes.

A few minutes later, a lone mouse charged down the corridor, threw a frightened glance over one shoulder, and was gone.

Silence.

Sounds of fighting exploded from the end of the tunnel, gathered intensity, and grew closer.

Four rats loped past the alcove where DeStra hid, their scarred faces grinning. Their fur, coated in foul-smelling oil, reeked of raw sewage. Their voices mingled down the hallway.

"Havik! Where is it?"

"Dunno."

"Boss said it would be here."

"What's he know anyway? I don't see it."

"I'll tell him you said that. He'll give you a nice War Claw tattoo."

"Shove off!"

"Har har har."

"Here. Found it."

"Get back, scum! This is my job. The boss gave it to me. I'm to pull the lever."

"Get on with it, then."

DeStra knew what they'd found. They were going

to trip the wall stone, leaving her trapped in the Commons.

She couldn't fight them, or run past them. And she mustn't risk staying where she was; when they returned they wouldn't be in a hurry, and the alcove was easier to see when one came east down the tunnel.

"Mousies thinks they's clever."

"Stuff it, LooGo."

"Har. And why should I?"

"So I don't bite your head off and spit it into the river."

"Go ahead, Havik. I haven't seen a head chewed off all day."

"They won't think they're clever when BlaKote's crew joins us at the east gate. I can see their mousey king now. 'Lemme in! Lemme in! Lemme in!' Har har har. Won't the boss have somepin' to say back?"

From down the corridor came a long, deep grunt, and then a loud thud as the wall stone slipped into its grooves and slammed into the tunnel floor.

DeStra took a deep breath and dove into the corridor, running blindly east into the Commons.

"Havik, look. No, that way."

"Mousey."

"Sport!"

Havik's voice raised above the others, lashing the air with whip-like fury. "No. Come back here, scum. Come back!"

DeStra ran east. South. East again. Through darkness, around corners of rounded clay and down alleys as silent and empty as graves.

In the open she could never have outrun them. But she was used to moving through the maze of tunnels, and knew this section of the city.

Chest heaving, she stopped in the entry of an unlit chamber-hole in the southwest corner of the Commons. She listened for the sound of pursuit.

Nothing.

Gradually, her breathing slowed, and she began to believe she must have evaded them.

Then something reached out of the darkness from behind her and clamped a paw over her mouth, silencing her scream.

36
Blang

Clogged by stones and loose sticks, the connecting tunnel ended at an unexpected new wall. The Great Hall rang with shrieks of terror as fleeing civilians realized that the last exit from the Commons had been sealed. They wrung their paws in despair. They begged and pleaded for the barricade to be removed.

Blang ignored them. He knew what had to be done to save Tira-Nor. He understood the terrible genius of the rat master and saw with sickening clarity the danger that threatened the city.

Had the kingsguard remained in the city, such an attack could have been met swiftly. But then, had the kingsguard remained in the city, militia would not have been posted at the gate holes, and the rats wouldn't have gained entry in the first place.

But how did the rats know when to attack? Or

where? Or how?

The loss of one gate might be put down to luck. The loss of every gate could only mean someone had betrayed Tira-Nor.

Blang would have to hold at least one gate open for the return of the kingsguard. Otherwise, the helpless commoners would be massacred.

The Wind Gate in particular inspired his fear. That entrance above all others must be protected until the kingsguard arrived.

He listened as the howling from the north end of the Great Hall intensified.

"Platoon Four!" he shouted. Ten faces gathered around him. He led them through the billets south of the Great Hall. They ran into the southwest corridor, and from there into the perimeter tunnel that would spiral up into the gate complex of the Wind Gate.

Behind them, the clatter of confusion died away and was replaced by an eery quiet. Blang heard himself breathing as he ran, the sound of his lungs drawing air, his paws pounding the hardened earth of the tunnel floor.

They rounded a corner, took the coiled spine of the tunnel at a sprint where it sloped upward into the elevated mound of the Wind Gate.

From the green, glowstone-lit gloom ahead of them came a scream and a whistle. The alarm, cut short by a cheer that could only have come from the raspy throats of a rat-pack.

A shadow leapt into Blang with crushing impact. He turned, hit the ground, saw one of the militia-mice leap beyond him and into the waiting trap of another rat. Blang raked with his hind legs, shot a forepaw into the chin of his attacker. He heard a low grunt.

The second rat caught him across the cheek with its claws, drawing long gashes across the scabs left by SoSheth. Blang ducked and moved in, elbowed the second rat in the stomach. He crushed its left knee with a slashing kick. The rat yelped, and Blang rolled away, pressing his back against the wall. He needed the wall at his back, needed a moment to evaluate so he could move forward into the Gate Complex. The tunnel curved, and he could not see beyond the few paces that lay before him. He did not know how many rats lurked there, but he knew the Wind Gate must be held. He would have to defend the alcove housing the trip lever to the wall stone.

"Forward!" he shouted. "Forward!"

He staggered on, saw a fist of movement rolling down thunderously from another tunnel that emptied into the main corridor. Four rats, maybe more. He could not see behind them, did not know how deep their ranks went.

He willed himself not to retreat, to hold the point of the line so his militia would stand behind him.

The truth punched him in the gut. He was alone!

His militia mice had not followed him. An urge to turn and look swept over him. Had any of his sudden-soldiers followed him into the breach? Or were the rats closing in behind him?

But he didn't look. He couldn't, for even now the rats were upon him.

Planning to die with his teeth in its throat, Blang picked the foremost rat as his target and launched himself at its great bulk. They collided with stunning impact. He heard a crack, realized that a bone had broken, but felt no pain. He clawed at the rat's face, but more bodies spilled into the ever-constricting knot of the passage.

Mice. His mice.

They had not run after all. They poured in behind him, meeting the rat attack with a ferocity that astonished him.

Paws lifted him up and helped him stand. Whatever bone he had broken must not have been his. He pressed on, over the struggling bodies, all thoughts blotted out by the one goal. He must reach the alcove. He must keep the Gate open for the Kingsguard's return.

He rounded another corner and saw a mass of rat tails, oiled fur, and blood-smeared bodies.

In spite of himself, Blang hesitated. The alcove lay beyond them.

He heard a sound like a great wind, felt the floor

tremble, and even the rats turned to look over their shoulders as the trip lever snapped into place.

The great wall stone shuddered in its grooves, thundering to the floor so heavily that he felt the impact of it in the flat of his rear paws.

He had failed.

The gate was closed.

The mice of the Commons were trapped.

37

DeStra

"Shhhh," a voice whispered. "The rats are every-where. Can't be too careful."

The paw over DeStra's mouth drew back. She turned to stare into the darkness. "KahEesha?"

"Shhhh!"

They waited.

Finally, "Are you all right, DeStra?"

"I came to get you out. Where's everyone else?"

"I don't know. Father and KeeRed had scavenging duty."

"They're safe then. They'll have gone in through the Royal Gate by now."

"You shouldn't have risked coming here. You were better off in the Families."

"Not my fault. I came to warn you about the rats, but I ran into one of their patrols!"

KahEesha sighed and pulled DeStra deeper into the

ReDemec home. "You're lucky to be alive. We'll have to go somewhere else to wait this thing out. I was just about to leave when I caught sight of the rats heading this way, and then you popped in."

"I can take care of myself."

Her tone softened. "I am glad not to be alone." She led DeStra into a distant sleeping chamber and picked up a bundle in the darkness, cooing.

"How is he?" DeStra stroked the downy new fur between Norrie's ears.

"Sleeping, fortunately. We'll have to move quietly."

"Where to?"

"The escape tunnel."

DeStra shook her head. The tunnel had once been an intricate architectural masterpiece, designed to require no sentry. Besides being a secret, its series of pits, hooks, and other booby traps made navigating its length next to impossible. Last summer JaRed collapsed the tunnel at the ancient room of the rock and pillar. A place known as The Chamber of Wroth. She shivered. "Isn't that a dead end?"

"Yes. But they aren't likely to search it for some time. If what you told me about Kreeg is correct, he doesn't have the numbers. Especially since they don't know which passages are trapped."

"It isn't just Kreeg," DeStra said. "The rats that chased me mentioned reinforcements. And a name.

BlaKote. They were going to hook up at East Gate.

KahEesha cupped her chin with one paw. "Kreeg has closed all the gates except one. He's going to bring in reinforcements."

"Yes."

"Unless someone stops him."

DeStra nodded. "I'll need you to create a diversion while I climb into the alcove and pull the lever."

KahEesha looked down at the sleeping kit in her arms. Gently, she kissed his forehead and placed him back in the fur-lined pallet of her sleeping chamber.

A whistle split the air. Shrill, piercing, it cleaved the stillness of the Commons and rebounded off the tunnel walls.

"Whatsat?" a rat from the guard chamber said. "Did it sound like a mousey?"

There was a long pause, then: "Whadid boss say? 'E said not to let mousies in. Anee said not to eat somepin. Diden say Mangey coulden ava looksee, didee?"

DeStra drew deeper into the shadows. Light from the moon dusted the edges of the corridor in the twisting network of tunnels that comprised the East Gate complex.

She listened, hardly daring to breathe.

Snarls from the guard chamber. "So maybe I munna ava looksee." His shadow blotted the dim light from the end of the tunnel, and his foul-smelling body passed inches from her nose.

She stifled a gasp.

The rat stopped. "Noowwww ..." he said. "Which waydee go, mousey?" He sniffed, a long, low breath through open nostrils. "That way." His steps pattered away down the corridor, and DeStra was left alone.

She stepped into the tunnel and hurried the twenty paces in semi-darkness, her heart pounding, her ears open for the sound of footsteps. From the guard chamber came the dull greenish light of a fading glow stone. DeStra half-wished her destination lay on the far side of the chamber, for afterward she could leave through the open gate hole and return above ground to the Families.

But no. The alcove loomed ahead of her on the right.

She felt the ledge in the wall with the fingers of her right paw. She leapt into the alcove and groped about in the darkness.

The wooden lever protruded from the floor like the trunk of a small tree, ending in a smooth round shaft that felt cool to the touch. She took a deep breath and tugged on the lever. It didn't budge.

She pulled again, harder this time. She leaned back, pulling with all her weight. A grunt escaped her lips, loud in the silence. She braced her legs against the floor, kicked back against the wall in front of her for leverage. She strained. Blood pounded in her temples.

"Whatsit doin?" Rat paws grabbed her ankles.

DeStra screamed. Unrestrained, full of dread and cold hatred. She struggled with all her might, but her legs were pinned.

"Bad mousey," the rat said, and pulled.

Clutching the lever, she fell. Her paws slid down the length of it, splinters slicing into her fingers, her palms. She tightened her grip. Her face struck the floor.

She heard a sharp crack. Her hands and her face were on fire. The earth groaned, shuddered.

The wall stone fell.

38

SoSheth

King SoSheth ran until his lungs burned. He ran until the sweat dripped from his face in rivulets, until the muscles in his legs, back, and neck begged him to quit, until the ache of his limbs dulled and became meaningless.

He lost track of time. He seemed to be outside himself, watching his body run through shadow and frost. The path hooked left and then descended into a glade rimmed by oaks. He recognized it. Beyond the glade the ground rose and then fell away to the west.

The ache and throb of his body returned. He was home. Tira-Nor lay over the next rise.

It occurred to him that he should go no farther until some of his mice caught up with him. There were rats in Tira-Nor. A battle raged there even now. And he had neither the troops nor the physical strength to join the battle.

He stopped, panting.

At some point, others from the kingsguard would catch up to him. They had scattered, therefore they would return home. They would come here. For the moment, he must wait.

He leaned against the base of a tree and tried to stop himself from shaking.

—⟨∞⟩—

"It's closed, your highness."

"Closed?" SoSheth glared at Lieutenant FaLin.

"By a wall stone."

The lieutenant and ten other kingsguard mice were all that remained of his two hundred warriors. No stragglers had joined them in over an hour, though the afternoon sun was stooping over the horizon. They would have to take their chances now. "We can't just wait out here in the open."

"The southern gates of the Commons are sealed off. I don't know yet about the Families and Kings-guard. I sent runners to the other gates, but it doesn't look good."

SoSheth cursed. Closed gates meant more than temporary delays. They meant unanswered questions. Multiplied headaches, rebuilding problems, and—much worse—the real possibility of a prolonged fight in the tunnels underground.

He cursed Captain YaGo. He cursed Captain Blang.

He cursed TaMir, Tira-Nor, and ElShua. He even cursed the late General LaRish for being dead at a most inopportune time. Most of all, he cursed the runt.

FaLin's eyes drew wide at the last explosion of violent hatred. He stared beyond SoSheth as though realizing something for the first time. Then, with unbelievable audacity, the lieutenant jumped forward and struck SoSheth to the ground.

SoSheth stood a head taller than most of the kingsguard, and FaLin himself was no small mouse. But the king was unprepared for the blow. He tumbled backward, shock momentarily suppressing anger. He rose with his back to the hole of the closed gate.

FaLin crouched into a defensive posture. Before SoSheth could make sense of what happened, a rat appeared. An Ur'Lugh rat. Eyes black and dripping hatred. A coat of oily dark fur, and a face scarred by many sewer brawls.

The rat struck FaLin in the throat. The blow brought FaLin's paws to his neck and dropped him to the ground.

SoSheth froze. *FaLin's shove saved my life.*

The rest came as a blur. SoSheth attacked even as Lieutenant FaLin gagged his life away on the hard cold soil of the prairie.

The Ur'Lugh rat backed away from the force of SoSheth's anger, but more rats appeared, spilling over the banks of Dry Gully in a disciplined and therefore terrifying line. More Ur'Lugh. At least thirty of them, perhaps as many as fifty, and SoSheth had nowhere to run. With the gate closed, there wasn't room in the narrow alcove of the tunnel mouth to make a defensive stand. SoSheth and his ten kingsguard would have to fight in the open.

He shouted the command for a Wall of Teeth, and those kingsguard who remained drew inward and formed a circle around him. Nine mice and their king. This was what remained of his kingdom. This was all that could be mustered outside the once-proud City of Promise to defend their Lord and the Known Lands.

He spat, scowling at the rats charging into the battle. *Let me die facing my enemy at the last!* For though he felt a terror born of the certainty of death, at least it was a familiar terror, something to fuel combat, something to make him strong to bite, claw, and kill. Something to help him die as a warrior.

He shouldered his way into the line between two fear-rattled mice. "We are the kingsguard. Let's give them something to remember us by!"

Then the rat line hit them, and SoSheth lost himself in the nightmare of battle, the mindless horror of attack and defense.

The kingsguard line broke, as he had known it would. There were no reserves to plug the gaps. In the open, the rats could attack from every direction at once. Soon, the knot of fighting mice broke into a confused mass of twisting, clawing bodies.

SoSheth dispatched three of the brutes in the late afternoon glory of the setting sun. In return he took a number of superficial bites, a nasty cut to the leg, and a bone-shattering blow to his ribs that speared his lungs with a pain so vast he thought it would never end.

The rescue force that came for them numbered less than a dozen mice. He did not hear who sounded the attack, but he saw them coming. Rushing from the West Gate in a charge so proud he smiled in spite of himself just to see it. A handful of mice, good mice, mice of the palace kingsguard—their fur streaming back, their tails straight as arrows, their eyes blazing with ferocity, all of them intent on saving their king. They shot onto the battlefield in a coordinated attack. And at their head, leading them ...

Prince JoHanan.

My son.

Tears flooded his eyes. *You can't win this one. You can't save me. Go back!*

But he knew JoHanan would not turn back, would not and could not save either of them. Insistently, mockingly, a voice twisted inside King SoSheth's head. *"Death, my lord! Death! Death is the most powerful magic there is!"*

JoHanan came on. The palace kingsguard collided

with the main force of the Ur'Lugh, which buckled, bent, and nearly collapsed in the center. The rat line gave. It heaved, and SoSheth took an expectant breath. To the west, the sun slid into the trees, hurling shadows across the surface of the open field. Rats wrapped themselves around the new mouse warriors, attacking with renewed strength.

SoSheth fought off one rat, then two more, shoving, biting, no longer himself, but a void inside a doomed body.

He tried to get through to his son. Oh, how he tried! Into his last, most desperate attack, he thrust all of his pent-up rage and disgust and self-loathing. He had been wrong about his son, and that knowledge was a fearsome force indeed. He had despised JoHanan as weak, when the boy was not weak. He had belittled him as a traitor, when his son remained a loyal ally. He had rejected JoHanan as a poor heir, but the prince was a good heir. And now ... now it was too late.

He could not break the rat line.

The fighting ended abruptly. The rats drew back, gathering to see the king's final moment. They must have wanted his pain to linger, and no wonder. They had paid dearly for it.

JoHanan lay unnaturally still.

SoSheth stumbled to him, his voice cracking, his limbs beyond exhaustion. "JoHanan!" he cried. "My son!"

Prince JoHanan's eyes remained fixed on the horizon.

"JoHanan ... JoHanan ... my son!" SoSheth gathered the body in his paws, heedless of the pain in his side, the mocking laughter of the rats, his own impending doom. "Listen to me. Listen to your father, your king. Listen. You will be a good king. You will. You aren't a disgrace to me. I'm not ashamed. I don't want a different heir. JoHanan ... JoHanan!"

With the gentleness of a mother comforting a newborn babe, King SoSheth rocked on his heels, cradling the body in his arms.

He closed his eyes when the rats drew in around him.

The sun fell behind the black shroud of the horizon.

39

JaRed

"I don't like it." JaRed stood just inside the shadowed edge of the Dark Forest and peered west across the prairie toward the mound of Round Top. Soon stars would begin popping through the black curtain of night.

Black shapes swayed in the distance on the crest of Dry Gully and then disappeared. Closer, but still some distance from where he and the Grenadiers stood watching, little earthen mounds lay like stones.

Gibbs sucked his teeth. "Afraid I'm not much help. Haven't seen Tira-Nor before. Don't know what to expect."

"It's too quiet. And there are bodies outside the Open Gate."

Gibbs chewed thoughtfully on that information, his eyebrows drawn into a long arch.

"And there." JaRed pointed to Dry Gully. "Do you

see shadows in the dead grass?"

Gibbs squinted. "I see something."

"A rat patrol. An ambush. They're set up to hit anyone approaching a gate-hole on the western edge of the city. Those are the gates used by the Families, the Kingsguard, and the Palace. My guess is the gates to the Commons are closed. Kreeg expects us to try to get in through the Commons, and to keep moving west until we find an open hole. That would give the rats in Dry Gully a clear view of our numbers and leave them in perfect position to tear us to pieces."

Gibbs looked at JaRed with an expression of mild astonishment. He said cheerfully, "but of course, this General Kreeg fellow couldn't have known his rats would be facing Grenadiers, could he?"

JaRed smiled. "At least the whole city hasn't fallen yet. We still control the Kingsguard, the Families, and the Palace."

"And how can you possibly know that?"

"Two reasons. When I was in Kreeg's dungeon, the general had less than sixty fighters. With Blang defending the city, Wroth himself couldn't swallow all of it with so few."

"What if Blang is dead?"

"Then there's the second reason. If all of Tira-Nor has fallen, why would Kreeg bother setting an ambush? He could post sentries at the gates and gorge himself on the palace storerooms all winter long.

While we starve or freeze to death out here in the open."

"What shall we do, then, eh? Ambush or no, my lads are ready for a good spat. How many rats can there be anyway? Sixty? Seventy? There are thirty three of us. A bit lopsided, I admit. But if Kreeg can't find any more rats we can always leave a few Grenadiers behind to make it even."

JaRed stared at the open prairie for a long time. The shadows deepened. Stars crept across the sky. He chewed his lower lip. "Why don't you go home now, colonel? Back to West Exiter. You have my gratitude."

Gibbs's chin dropped. "Go?"

"Take the grenadiers and forget all of this. Your families will be missing you by now. You've done enough. I release you."

Gibbs stared at him. A scowl spread across his face. "You release us? We've done enough? You're off your cheese."

"I can't allow you to come with me."

"Do you understand what you're saying? We were sent to the king of Tira-Nor. That's you, JaRed. Like it or not. We can't leave you now. Especially now. Why else would the Badger have sent us if not to help you now?"

"The Badger?"

"You needn't look so shocked." Gibbs looked away.

"But, I thought—"

Gibbs shook his head. "He appeared three months ago. Rose up out of the ground and struck my second, Major Simmerson. One blow to the neck. Killed him instantly. Then turned those eyes to me. Irresistible. He said, 'The grenadiers must aid the king of Tira-Nor.' And just like that he was gone. When he said king I thought he meant, well." Gibbs cleared his throat. "Now I know he meant you."

"Are you telling me the Ghost-Badger—the thing that destroyed most of the kingsguard—is actually on our side?"

"Our side? Oh, no, JaRed. The Badger is not on our side. He answers to a higher master. But I would not want to be his enemy."

"He killed your second."

"Yes."

"Why?"

"I don't know. But I suspect. Well, one mustn't speak ill of the dead. But Simmerson would have been reluctant to support a mouse of your, shall we say, breeding. He was ever the aristocrat. No offense intended."

"There are now two kingdoms, and all must choose one or the other."

"Indeed." Gibbs beamed. "You were paying attention."

After a moment JaRed nodded. "Are you sure you want to go with me? It's probably suicide."

Gibbs arched his back. "Most astonishing bad form. Releasing us. That sort of thing won't do. You need us."

"I do."

"Glad to hear you've come to your senses. So what will it be, commander? A suicidal charge across the open prairie? Straight into the teeth of the enemy? A bloodbath that will live for centuries in the legends of our descendants?"

"Actually," JaRed said. "I have a better idea."

40

JaRed

JaRed climbed the slope of Round Top, scuttling from shadow to shadow until he stood at last on the narrow ledge above Dry Gully. Moonlight lay across the silent field, dampened here and there by dark ribbons of cloud drifting past.

Spread out in a long line below him, sheltered by the crest of the gully, the Ur'Lugh waited. They gazed at the empty field. Yawned. Scratched at fleas. One rat complained about being hungry. Another told it to shut up. A third picked at its teeth with a dirty claw.

Rat sentries lounged at either end of the gully, secure in their position. And why not? They could see the field above Tira-Nor clearly from where they waited. The black line of the Dark Forest posed no threat.

They are overconfident. JaRed smiled. *Good.*

Time passed. Many of the rats slept. The moon rose higher, brightening the crusted web of snow and grass that draped the field.

JaRed wished he'd told Gibbs to begin sooner, but he had not expected to climb Round Top so quickly.

Too late to do anything about it now. Tira-Nor was depending on him.

At last, a black shadow rose in the field, blurred to gray at the edges. It swayed as it rose, as though caught in a slow wind.

The sentries didn't notice it.

Asleep, most likely.

The shadow descended back to earth. A moment later it rose again. Swayed. Descended.

Maybe we should have tried the frontal assault after all. Might have caught them napping.

He picked up a stone and hurled it at the farthest sentry, aiming wide. It was a bad throw. He meant to miss. Instead, the rock caught the rat squarely in the nose, pitching it sideways. It stood with teeth bared, its head swiveling in all directions.

The shadow rose again, swaying impatiently. A voice carried across the field. "WHOOOO?"

The Ur'Lugh sentry's eyes widened. "Krum! You see that?"

The rats came alive. They poked their snouts over the crest of the gully, ready for a fight.

Their speed was disheartening. They were, after

all, Ur'Lugh. JaRed was glad he had chosen not to pit the Grenadiers against them in a contest of strength and speed.

"WHOOOO?" The shadow howled. "WHOOOO disturbs my rest? WHOOOO wakens the spirit of the king?"

"Whatsey mean?" a rat asked.

"What is it?"

"Looks like a mouse to me."

"All black?"

"Moon's behind it."

"It's the king! The one we killed!"

"Can't be."

"KINGSGUARD WARRIORS." The shadow shrieked. "AWAKEN. COME FORTH. FIND THE LIVING. BRING THEM TO ME!"

Around the shadow other shapes emerged, rising from grass and snow. Rounded stones quivered in the moonlight and jerked upright. They shook themselves and stood in long, awkward silhouettes. They formed two rows, teetering on unsteady legs. The foremost shadow pointed a black fist at the gully. The others turned in unison, every head snapping to face the Ur'Lugh. Slowly, they shambled forward.

"They're comin' back to life!"

"Hold the line, you slime," Krum bellowed. "Hold the line or I'll have your ears!"

JaRed's plan wasn't working. The Ur'Lugh leader

kept too much control over his crew. He would have to deal with Krum first. Then the huge rats on either side of him.

He took a deep breath to calm his nerves, and jumped. Speed-wind hissed its seashell song in a mad rush between his ears. He hit Krum's back with his hind legs, knocking the rat to the ground. He rolled, jumped, launched himself at the snarling brute to the right. Time slowed to an underwater crawl. He could not have said whether he fought for moments or hours.

He took a glancing blow to his face. He recovered, ducked, struck back. Claws ripped into his shins as he leaped out of the way. Pain, but nothing serious. Then a foul smell of oil and sewage as the monster flung itself at him. JaRed sidestepped and struck the rat's jaw. Its head snapped sideways and back, like a garden gate. The rat teetered, its eyes glazing, and collapsed.

JaRed looked around for another enemy, but the Ur'Lugh were gone.

The Grenadiers crested Dry Gully and stood on moon-pasted rocks. They grinned at him.

Someone said, "Well done, JaRed!"

"Knows how to pick a fight."

"Dropped that blighter like deadwood."

"Cunnel! Have you seen wot JaRed did?"

"Six of them, colonel!"

"Wot me old mum would 'ave called utter carnage."

"Didn't even break a sweat."

Laughter.

"Whoooo!" Gibbs howled. "Simply brilliant. We could have used you at the battle of Ford's Creek. That right, lads?"

Cheers.

JaRed waved away the compliments. "Grenadiers, I believe Tira-Nor would be grateful for our company."

41

Blang

Terrified civilians jammed the north end of the Great Hall. They pressed themselves into the wedge of the corridor, screaming, cursing, threatening.

The tunnel was closed. The palace kingsguard had barricaded it with stones, sticks, and piles of dirt.

Blang cursed himself for a fool. He cursed King SoSheth for leaving Tira-Nor defenseless. He cursed whoever was in charge on the other side of the barricade. Probably some pampered officer from the palace kingsguard. Whoever it was should have waited for all the fleeing civilians to come through before closing the corridor.

"MeerQo," he said. "How many mice do we have left?"

"Fourteen," MeerQo replied. "Ryn and GaVin returned twenty minutes ago. HarVik's platoon is gone."

"The rats will have moved by now. We'll be surrounded soon."

"Yes, sir."

"Any idea how many there are?"

"Sixty. Forty. A hundred." MeerQo shivered. "They're not normal rats, sir."

Blang knew what he meant. "They fight well, don't they?"

MeerQo looked at the blood on Blang's fur. Blang had suffered a number of minor cuts and bruises, all of which would hurt more later than they did now. But the damage seemed to encourage MeerQo. "Yes, sir. For rats."

"But we can't make our stand in the Great Hall. Not with so few." Blang looked around.

Eight tunnels opened into the massive underground chamber. One led to the kingsguard and was sealed. The three to the south led to the training hall of the militia, the Common Gate complex, and three major arteries into the southern section of the commons. To the east, two massive openings led to the largest of the city's underground tunnels. Two other tunnels opened on the west wall, one to the militia's barracks that lay between the Families and Commons, and one that led down to the lowest levels of the city. Blang made up his mind. "We'll have to move them somewhere more defensible. Wait here."

"Sir."

He turned his attention to the crowd. With grim determination he threw himself into the press of bodies. "Stand back. Make way. Move for the kingsguard!"

Though he no longer served in the kingsguard, the mice of the commons retained a healthy respect for his size and fighting ability. Some moved out of his way. He felt as though he were wading through a river of bodies, and he began to claw at them to get them to move. He used his great fists as bludgeons, and hurled a few of the more stubborn males behind him like great clods of dirt.

When he neared the mouth of the tunnel he saw that the crowd had succeeded in destroying part of the barricade. Three males were nosing into the dirt and sticks, chewing, scooping, shoveling the debris behind them onto the heads of their fellow civilians, heedless of the consequences. Blang cursed them for fools. As if in response, a lump of red clay struck him in the forehead and bounded off into the darkness. On the far side of the barricade, kingsguard mice stuffed the cleared hole with fresh dirt and small stones as quickly as the civilians removed it. Both sides hurled insults into the hole.

"STOP!" Blang made his voice huge. The voice of command. The voice he used in combat.

The mice at the hole stopped. One of them snarled, lips quivering with fear and rage. "Who are you?"

Blang recognized this one. A born troublemaker named DinGa. "You know who I am, DinGa son of GaBin." He turned in a circle, addressing the civilians with his most piercing stare. "Listen to me! The militia can't hold the Great Hall. There are too many entrances. But we can hold the barracks. You must all follow MeerQo into the billeting area at once. You'll be safe there. We can protect you. If you stay here you will die."

"Protect us?" DinGa spat. "It's your fault the rats got in! We're not going anywhere! We're going to chew through this barricade if it takes all day, and then we're going to kill the half-wits on the other side who are trying to keep us out. You go to your barracks if you like it so much!" He turned around and began to claw once more at the barricade.

The crowd hesitated. The instinct to obey was strong in them. But the instinct to flee was also strong, and here they stood closest to the last possible exit from the Commons. To enter the barracks would mean abandoning their only hope of getting out. Few trusted the militia to hold back the ferocity of the rats.

Blang shoved forward. The crowd, sensing his fury, fell away, forming a narrow path to the tunnel mouth.

DinGa must have sensed the danger, for he looked over one shoulder, gave a frightened squeal of terror, and renewed his efforts to open the hole. Dirt flew from the tunnel in a cloud.

Blang strode forward, reaching with outstretched claws.

MeerQo sounded a warning. "RATS!"

Screams. A mad press of bodies crushing against him. Blang struggled to turn, but was pushed backward into the tunnel.

The south end of the Great Hall cleared. MeerQo raced to where the other militia-mice stood waiting. Blang's militia formed a line at the south entrance. They were not fleeing. They meant to fight.

Pride swelled his chest, but he could not get to them.

He snarled. He cursed, threatened, began to snap with a fury so violent that one or two mice went down before him. He lashed out with open claws, began to pummel the stupid fools blocking his way. Before long, the flow of the crowd would be halted by the barricade.

The first rats appeared in the entrance to the training hall, shrieking threats. Behind MeerQo, four more slipped into the confusion of the Great Hall from the closest of the eastern tunnels to strike the militia from behind.

"MeerQo!" Blang shouted. "Behind you!"

Above the din, MeerQo heard. He turned at the last moment and saw the trap closing. He gave an order the mice quickly obeyed.

Retreat. Shield Wall. Protect the civilians.

Blang's militia hurled themselves back toward the crowd at the kingsguard tunnel. Ryn and two others collided with the rats between, and Blang lost sight of them. They spaced themselves shoulder-to-shoulder in groups of three, the last hope of the mice of the Commons.

Rats swaggered into the Great Hall. Ten. Twenty. Thirty.

They launched themselves at Blang's militia with a ferocity that sent new panic into the already terrified civilians.

One by one, the militia-mice went down.

Still the flow of bodies pressing into the tunnel didn't stop. Blang was carried ever closer to the barricade. The impossibility of this did not dawn on him until the current lost its momentum.

Fewer mice in the Great Hall. More dead bodies as the rats dispatched the last of the militia-mice and began to kill helpless civilians.

Blood. Terror. Screaming. A kit bawling for its mother.

Blang stood like an island now, and the mice flowed around him, away from the teeth that shredded the crowd's flanks.

Somehow DinGa prevailed. The barricade collapsed, and mice escaped into the kingsguard section of Tira-Nor.

After what seemed an eternity, Blang forced his way to the mouth of the tunnel. He bellowed his war cry and took a defensive fighting posture as the last of the surviving civilians bounded past him into the tunnel.

The rats pressed closer in a vast semi-circle.

Blang wanted nothing more than this moment. It was a good day to die, and this a good place to do it. Here he had a narrow space to defend; the rats must attack him one at a time.

"Cowards!" he shouted. "Filthy rat cowards. Come and taste a real enemy!"

In the black circle of the tunnel mouth, few rats seemed to relish the idea of facing him in single combat.

They hissed, drew closer, hesitated.

The last of the civilians wiggled through the hole behind him, leaving a lonely emptiness at his back.

He sensed the palace kingsguard filling in the hole behind him, sealing him in his fate, but he did not care. The fall of Tira-Nor did not rest on the cruelty of rats, but on his own blind stupidity. It was his fault alone. He had sealed the fate of the Commons the day he let TaMir die.

All he could hope for now was atonement.

He stood tall, clenching his teeth. "Which of you?" he snarled. "Which of you wants to die first?"

42

JaRed

JaRed squinted in the underworld darkness. Light from a dying glowstone cast shadows in the familiar tunnel.

Sergeant Shoop, an aging mouse with hunched shoulders and close-set eyes, pursed his lips into a thin smile. "Never thought I'd say it, but I'm glad to see you."

"I'm not alone," JaRed said. "I've brought friends."

One by one, the Grenadiers ducked through the gate hole behind him.

Gibbs saluted. "Colonel Gibbs, Fourth Infantry, Light, of the Kings Royal Grenadiers, West Exiter. We've heard much about Tira-Nor. Most pleased to make your acquaintance."

"Friends of JaRed is friends of us," Shoop said. "And by the Owl some of us knows it now."

A handful of older kingsguard warriors appeared in

the shadows: Grouser, Stubs, Del, HenRi, DrinIn, Kurt.

"Heard you were in a bit of a bind," Gibbs said.

"Consarned rats took the Commons." Grouser chewed the wiry stubs of whisker along his snout. "We're all that's left of the kingsguard, but you can count on us. We're with you."

JaRed should have made the introductions, but he couldn't speak. He felt as though someone had punched him in the gut.

He brushed past Grouser and Shoop, deeper into Tira-Nor. The others followed him.

Mice lined the corridor. Refugees from the Commons, haggard and bleeding, eyes weary. Kits whined for home and were hushed. Old mice cleared their throats and looked away, despair drawing their faces into long masks.

"Not that it's my place to say so," Shoop said as they descended, "but there's no end of bickering among the nose-dabbers in the Families. YuLooq declared himself provisional ruler less than an hour ago."

"YuLooq?"

"The old wart," Grouser muttered, "doesn't know his backside from his brain. Not that there's much difference."

"And there's still the rats to deal with," Shoop said. "We figure there's fifty or sixty holed up in the Commons."

"What about Blang?"

Shoop shook his head. "Died defending the Great Hall."

JaRed stopped in the tunnel. Mice stared at him.

Blang dead?

Impossible.

Fury started a slow burn in JaRed's cheeks. "Who's in charge now?"

Shoop seemed surprised. "Well. I suppose you are."

"Me?"

"You're the only officer left."

Grouser nodded. "It'll be different now. You can count on that. With SoSheth and JoHanan both dead, we figure—"

"JoHanan?"

Grouser cleared his throat. "Thought you knew. Anyway, there's no one else. And we want you to know you can count on us. All of us that's left from the old kingsguard. There's still some fight left in these claws."

JaRed pressed one paw to his forehead. "I appreciate that. Thank you. But ... what do you expect me to do?"

"Do?" Grouser asked. "Haven't you been listening?"

Shoop motioned for Grouser to be quiet. "Maybe we ought to do this in the palace."

"Do what?"

"Might be more room there. Come on, JaRed."

Grouser took JaRed's elbow and nudged him forward.

All at once, JaRed understood. "You're going to make me king."

The older kingsguard mice exchanged meaningful looks. "TaMir's prophecy," said an ancient gray-hair.

Shoop spoke for the group. "Might be ElShua has left us. And it might be He brought us to this point for a reason. Might be He meant us to recognize His king."

JaRed's mouth hung open. He didn't want to be king. He had never wanted to be king. Not even when he saw the injustices inflicted on the mice of the Commons. Not even when King SoSheth ordered his exile and execution.

He shook his head to clear it, and brushed past them down the tunnel. "I don't believe it."

TaMir's voice spun in his mind as he walked, the old Seer's whisper striking sparks in the cold air of memory, heavy and majestic at the same time. *Someday they will all kneel as I do. JaRed ... You are the next king of Tira-Nor!*

The old warriors pattered after him, followed by a train of Grenadiers.

"We'll have the ceremony in the Palace Hall," Shoop said. "With witnesses from the Families so its done proper."

Me? King?

The stench of infection and death worsened as Ja-

Red slipped deeper into the tunnel. Horror overshadowed the joy of homecoming, punctuated the irony of kingship under such grim circumstances.

At the entrance to the Kingsguard section of Tira-Nor, the bodies lay in heaps. Dying mice clotted the guard chambers and spilled into the tunnel from the entry hole. A few compassionate souls moved among them, stopping here and there to whisper words of comfort.

JaRed passed through the narrow space, the knot in his throat tightening. He tried to look away from the corpses, but could not. Each lifeless stare came as a revelation.

He had seen this coming. He had seen these faces in his dreams. These bodies. These agonies. His nightmare had come to pass. He had not prevented it, after all.

King? How can I be king?

But it was the sign he was waiting for. The Promise. Proof that ElShua did not lie. That the Maker *was.*

Beyond the makeshift morgue, refugees stared at him from the barracks of the Kingsguard, though he barely noticed. He stopped at the tunnel mouth and stared.

A mouse sat there, her back against the tunnel wall, two dead kits on her lap, her paws moving over them mechanically.

264

"*I'm you. And Luk is GoRec! See my white?*"

"No." JaRed stood transfixed. "No no no."

"Come on, JaRed." Shoop touched JaRed's arm.

He couldn't move.

The mother looked up.

"*You didn't do it, did you?*"

She was grooming them for burial. Her dead kits were little wooden dolls, stiff and unmoving and perfect. No blood remained at their wounds. No dirt soiled the spotless fur. She had closed the eyes. Death touched only their mouths, which hung open accusingly.

"JaRed?" the mother whispered. "You're alive?"

Luk. Raz. The warrior kits.

"I. I didn't—"

Alive, yes. I fled Tira-Nor and left your kits to fend for themselves.

"You know," she said, "they wanted so much to be like you. JaRed Ratbane. King of Tira-Nor."

He stretched out one hand, his fingers trembling. Rage and sorrow battled for control.

King?

TaMir ... Why didn't you prepare me for this?

"King," Shoop said.

Understanding settled over the crowd. The word filled the tunnel and great chambers of the kingsguard like a sigh. Relief passed from face to face.

One by one, the mice of the commons knelt. They

bowed their heads. Their knees dimpled the straw-carpeted floor.

Slowly, painfully, the old warriors stooped to one knee. In the long and awkward silence, Grouser's lower lip twitched. Shoop pressed his fingers to his eyes.

"Why not have the ceremony here?" Grouser asked, his voice crackling.

"JaRed Ratbane," the mother repeated in wonder. "King of Tira-Nor."

"Majesty," Shoop said. "We await your command."

"No."

Grouser looked up. Shoop's eyebrows knitted together.

"Not king," JaRed said. "Not like this."

"But—"

"No." Determination rose stubbornly in his heart.

If ElShua would make me king, then so be it. But let it be ElShua who makes it happen.

JaRed turned to face the kneeling mice. "There will be no talk of kingship until the rats are defeated."

43

Kreeg

"Uh, boss," WoKot said. "Skulker tells me we lost the East Gate."

Kreeg turned on his lieutenant. "What do you mean?"

"Well. Seems someone tripped that wall stone too."

Kreeg stared. The East Gate was the only open gate. The only exit. The only way he could communicate with the Ur'Lugh to coordinate their attack. It was his only hope of reinforcements, his only line of retreat.

Which meant a protracted, bloody, and uncertain fight underground. And all the while the mice would be getting stronger, and he would be getting weaker. For somewhere out there were two hundred kingsguard warriors who might show up at any time.

Kreeg seethed. "Someone? What do you mean, someone?"

"Two someones, boss. Mice."

"Bring them to me."

WoKot snapped his fingers, and a rat left to fetch the mouse-vermin. "Actually, chief, they're both females."

"So? I'll kill them both."

"What do we do about the gate hole?"

Kreeg thought for a moment. "Dig a new one. Go around the stone."

"Won't be easy, boss."

"Just do it!"

A pair of scumdevils dragged the female mice into the chamber. "Eh, mousey?" one said, "Why so squirmey? Whatsit want with a big stone?"

Kreeg's eyes popped in their sockets, then narrowed. He approached DeStra slowly. "I told you what would happen the next time I saw you." He flicked War Claw out in one liquid motion and stuck the point under her chin.

She closed her eyes, gave a whimper of terror.

"WoKot?"

"Yes, chief?"

"How many women and little tikes have we captured here in this fine city of Tira-Nor?"

"That would be ... um, two, boss."

"Find me some others if you can," Kreeg said. "Unmarked, unharmed. And get the crew started on that exit."

FORTY THREE

Kreeg pressed the point of War Claw into the soft fur of DeStra's neck. "You remember War Claw, don't you?"

She didn't nod, but her eyes revealed that she understood.

"Good. Then you won't make any sudden movements." He drew her toward the Great Hall with the point of the claw. "I'd hate to lose my first hostage prematurely."

44

DeStra

DeStra stumbled and fell in the corridor. A rat kicked her, then jerked her up with one massive arm.

"Aww," the rat mocked, its breath like rotten cabbage. "Didums fall?"

KahEesha threw DeStra a sympathetic glance.

They plodded on until they reached the cavernous Great Hall.

Mice lay in heaps at the north end, stiffened under death's grip.

Kreeg grinned and turned in a circle. "We did it, WoKot. My plan worked."

"Sure did, boss. Clogged the tunnels with mousies. Kept their fighters away from the battle until it was too late."

"BlaKote wouldn't have thought of that."

"Nope."

"Nor GoRec."

"Not a chance."

"Where's their leader?"

WoKot pointed to the north end of the hall. "We finished him a few minutes ago. He killed some good scumdevils."

Kreeg snarled happily. "Wish I could have seen his face when he heard we were tripping the wall stones. Trapped in his own tomb. Ha!"

DeStra fought for air. *Blang dead? Impossible!* She looked at KahEesha, who's face went very pale. *Poor Kah!*

"But this was too easy!" Kreeg's tongue flicked out to lick his lips. "GoRec—may his soul rot for-ever—tried to take this place by force. When all that was needed was cunning." He stopped in front of Kah-Eesha, who turned her head away as tears began to spill down her cheek. "What's wrong, pretty? Fright-ened?"

KahEesha looked up at him, her face hardening. "Disgusted."

Kreeg laughed. "Doesn't like my manners. Isn't that a shame?"

But DeStra couldn't bear to watch the torment any longer. She spat at the gloating rat, then said, her voice full of venom, "You killed her husband."

"Did I?"

DeStra nodded toward the pile of bodies, her chin

held high. "It only took, what, thirty of you?"

Kreeg's voice flowed smooth as buttermilk. "You're awfully smug for a hostage. We've won, mousey."

"You've killed. You haven't won. You'll never make it out of Tira-Nor alive."

"Oh?" Kreeg hooted. He turned to WoKot. "D'ya hear that? We're doomed!" He came closer to DeStra, his melon-seed eyes boring into her. "And why is that? Who's to stop us from doing what we like? You? Your king? Your little runt hero?" He reached out with War Claw and brushed the velvety fur behind her left ear.

DeStra shivered.

"Your king is dead. Your hero is dead. Soon, you'll be dead. And we'll be eating from Tira-Nor's storerooms until spring. City of Promise. More like City of Fools."

"ElShua," KahEesha said.

Kreeg twitched at the sound.

"ElShua will save the city."

"Your God is dead too. Or we wouldn't be here."

But KahEesha had regained her composure, and she spoke with a confidence that clearly aggravated the rat. "ElShua is alive. And neither you nor GoRec nor any of your rat army can change that."

"This God of yours. Have you ever seen Him? Ever heard Him speak? Ever felt His touch on your skin?" He brushed the back of War Claw against KahEesha's cheek.

Behind the rat general, WoKot sniffed.

"Well?" Kreeg said. "Have you?"

As KahEesha's silence stretched into an answer, Kreeg smiled and turned to walk away. His face took on the squat features of a toad. "I thought not."

"Yes," KahEesha said, her voice defiant.

Unbelief drew a sneer across Kreeg's snout. "Yes, what?"

"I have. Heard his voice."

Kreeg padded the few paces to where KahEesha stood. He held aloft War Claw as though balancing an egg on its tip. "Well, then. By all means, tell us what he said. No, wait! Let me guess." He closed his eyes. "I, General Kreeg, am preordained to be the next king of Tira-Nor?"

WoKot laughed. Behind him, rats snorted in derision. "Har har har! Good one, boss!"

Kreeg rested the back edge of War Claw against KahEesha's throat. "Well? Out with it. I don't like to be kept waiting. What did ElShua tell you?"

"You mock," KahEesha said. "Therefore I won't tell you."

Kreeg's face flushed. "I think you will."

DeStra leaned forward, straining against the rat paws holding her back. "Please don't hurt her!"

Kreeg cast a sideways glance at her. He whispered to KahEesha, "What did your God tell you?"

KahEesha lifted her chin as though to present

Kreeg a larger target.

Trembling, DeStra said, "I know what ElShua told her. I do. I know. He said the future of Tira-Nor belongs to her. To KahEesha." Her voice sounded hollow. Thin. Far away.

KahEesha's jaw clenched.

"Did he?"

"Yes."

WoKot, whose gaze had wandered among them as they spoke, spat on the packed earth of the hall. "That's inspirational, boss."

"Well." Kreeg grinned. "If that's true, then I shouldn't be able to do this ..." His finger moved. A gentle tap. War Claw flicked in an arc, then seemed not to have moved at all.

KahEesha gasped, an indrawn breath like a hiccup, her lower jaw swinging down as her eyes narrowed. A tiny sliver of blood squeezed in a line across her throat. "Des..." Her eyes rolled back, the lids fluttering like a moth's wings over her cheeks.

DeStra screamed.

"Tell me something," Kreeg said as his grin stretched across his snout. "Where is ElShua now?"

45

JaRed

JaRed squinted through a hole in the barricade sealing off the Commons. "Kreeg?"

"This one here," the general said, "is a real beauty. You might remember her, Runt. Shared your corner of my dungeon."

"Let her go," JaRed said into the hole.

"Ah, well. I could do that. But then, what would we do for fun?"

Laughter from the rats. What they called sport.

"The fun would be surviving, general. If you free the hostages and agree to go peacefully, we will allow you to leave, one at a time, under escort."

"Allow us? Ho ho!" Kreeg hooted. "Do ya hear that, scumdevils? Mousey says he'll allow us to leave. Under escort. If we promise to play nice."

The rats snorted their disapproval.

"How about this, Runt. You and the rest of your

little mousey friends clear out of Tira-Nor now and we promise not to come looking for you in the forest. For a few hours."

More hoots from the rats.

"Since you disliked the Ur'Lugh," JaRed said, "it will not surprise you to hear that they have abandoned their posts and retreated to the sewers."

This cut short the laughter. Whispers filled the hall. Snarls of denial.

"Good," Kreeg said. "That's fewer mouths to feed."

"Also, the bridge is gone. I destroyed it myself."

"Dat's a lie, chief," a rat said. "No mousey could do that."

"All the more reason for us to stay," Kreeg said.

"Perhaps. But you've got, what, thirty rats left? We outnumber you, general. And I can't help wondering how long the coat of poison on War Claw will last."

Kreeg drew a rasping breath.

JaRed let the revelation sink in, then said, "You can't go back to your dresser drawer now, general. No more trips to the skull jar. So how many kills do you think you have left?"

Kreeg drew DeStra closer to the barricade and stood in the mouth of the connecting tunnel. DeStra remained erect, frozen by Kreeg's claw at her throat.

"Listen, scum! I'm the rat master. With or without War Claw, I'm a match for any of you. Tira-Nor is mine. ElShua has forgotten you. GET OUT OF MY

CITY!"

But at that moment, from the far, southern end of the Great Hall, came the battle cry of the Grenadiers.

Kreeg's head snapped around. He drew back into the tunnel, his back to JaRed, War Claw still hovering at DeStra's neck.

Mice erupted into the vast chamber. Gibbs, Dimble, and the rest of the Grenadiers, plus a handful of older kingsguard mice, their faces lit with vengeful fury, emerged from the western tunnels. Shoop and the mice of the Commons had worked for hours to clear the barricades in the connecting tunnels at the lowest levels of the city.

JaRed turned to the mice behind him. "Help me clear this hole. Now!" Without waiting for a response, he tugged a stone from the barricade and flung it aside.

In the Great Hall, Kreeg's crew gave way. The mice who tore into them were no mere civilians. They were muscular balls of fur, teeth, and claw, who seemed to know no pain, who moved like weasels and struck like wasps. Worse, they fought as a unit.

"Faster!" JaRed shouted, his front paws scratching at the opening. "Get me in there." Mice pressed around him, tore at the barricade with bleeding fingers.

Kreeg screamed orders. His rats were scrappy fighters, each bigger than any mouse. They fought with that recklessness for which rats are known when they are cornered.

The hole widened slowly. Over and over JaRed bellowed for the mice to hurry, to work faster, to get out of his way.

The battle lasted only a few minutes. Time enough for Leftenant Dimble to go down with a torn throat. Time enough for seven Grenadiers and Sergeant Shoop to die while JaRed watched helplessly.

But rats died too, one by one, and without hope.

JaRed reached into the opening and ripped away a stick. The hole was just big enough for his shoulders. The other mice would not be able to follow him through for some time, but that hardly mattered.

Kreeg watched from the tunnel mouth. His gaze darted here and there, wide and unbelieving and desperate. When WoKot died before him, Kreeg didn't utter a sound. Even when WoKot's last words gushed out in four futile spurts. "Almost ... worked ... eh ... boss?"

JaRed wiggled through the hole and dropped into a fighting stance.

Kreeg wrapped one arm around DeStra's neck and jammed War Claw into her jugular.

JaRed nodded toward the Grenadiers. "They won't interfere. You have my word."

"Your word?"

"Colonel Gibbs, you are not to interfere."

Private Collins stepped closer. "But JaRed!"

Kreeg's eyes narrowed.

"Let her go," JaRed said.

"And?"

"Fight me. One on one."

"Why?"

"Prove yourself. Prove that ElShua has left us. Prove your point."

Kreeg snorted and held out War Claw's curved blade. "This is my point."

"It is a weak point if it can't defend itself."

Kreeg scowled, pulled DeStra in tightly, and stuck War Claw under her left eye.

"Kill me," JaRed said, "and we'll allow you to leave."

DeStra gasped.

"Too bad, my pretty," Kreeg whispered. "Too bad you weren't born a rat."

He let her go.

DeStra shot JaRed a worried look.

He stepped forward and braced himself.

Kreeg's attack came like a whirlwind. Stillness followed by sudden fury. War Claw flicked out effortlessly, a wicked black needle slicing the air like the tail of a whip.

JaRed thought he was ready. He had settled himself into a low fighting stance, his right side forward, his weight balanced on all fours so he could move easily in any direction. Yet he staggered back under Kreeg's onslaught. He ducked, twisted, rolled, stood.

Kreeg kicked him in the ribs. JaRed struggled to evade the stabbing point of Kreeg's poisoned claw. He slashed at Kreeg's throat with the claws of his right paw, missed, blocked another blow with his forearm, and then spun toward the barricade, into the shadows.

Kreeg stood limed by the green light of the glow-stones that fired the Great Hall. He followed at Ja-Red's heels, his teeth gnashing, his claws reaching out for JaRed's flesh.

Kreeg was bigger, stronger, and had longer limbs. In such a fight, reach meant everything, for War Claw needed only one cut to kill.

JaRed retreated until he could go no farther. He evaded Kreeg's slashing cuts, wondering how he could use the narrow space to his advantage. The tunnel suited Kreeg more than JaRed.

He took a small cut on the left leg from the unpoisoned claws of Kreeg's left paw, felt a tug there, and then a brief sting. He kicked out at Kreeg's gut, heard a satisfying "Oof" as his heel connected with the rat's midsection. Then he jumped up and over, pinwheeling in the air, as Kreeg dove underneath in a failed attempt to cut JaRed's legs.

Now JaRed stood closest to the mouth of the tunnel, but this wasn't much better. Kreeg stood in shadow, and his movements would be harder to see.

"You're fast," Kreeg said, his chest heaving. "I'll give you that. But it doesn't matter. You're going to die anyway."

The general's words brought to focus a feeling that had been growing in JaRed since the beginning of the fight. A feeling that he could not win.

He shrugged, trying to portray an indifference he did not feel. "Maybe."

Kreeg spat a thin stream of saliva against the tunnel wall. "You're going in the ground. A shallow mouse-grave, where your body will rot and be eaten by mag-gots, and then turn back to dust, same as mine."

"You're sure of that?"

Kreeg spat again. "I've killed lots of mice, lots of rats. They all rot the same way." He leaped forward and swung War Claw in an arc that split the air with a wicked hiss.

JaRed dove to the floor, twisted, reached out with the claw of his right paw, and snagged the skin on the outside of Kreeg's right thigh. A shallow cut only.

War Claw bit JaRed's chest, parting the fur, the skin, drawing a gash sideways across his ribs in a line of red fire. Blood came to the surface and oozed down his stomach even as he rolled to all fours and backed away.

The burning sensation grew hotter, the cut a hot poker laid across his midsection, white-hot and sear-ing. He looked down, but Kreeg didn't bother to follow-up the attack with another.

The rat had won, and he knew it.

"There," he said. "Now I'm convinced."

The remaining Grenadiers gazed from JaRed to Kreeg, and from Kreeg back to JaRed. A sigh fell into the hushed silence of the tunnel. Disbelief stood on the faces of everyone.

"Suh?" Private Collins stepped forward out of line and glared at Kreeg. "Shall we attack this blighter?"

"No," JaRed said. "Stand back. Leave the general alone."

Collins turned to Gibbs. "But cunnel—"

"Private!" Gibbs growled. "Back in line."

JaRed sank to his knees. His voice clattered in his throat, as though he were falling ill. "Orders, remember?"

Kreeg stood in the shadows near the barricade, his gaze darting from JaRed to the other mice, his chest heaving. "You're no king, mousey." He flashed a triumphant smile. "You may be brave, but you're no king."

46

Kreeg

He almost couldn't believe his ears. The runt had kept his promise. *Insane!*

Not that Kreeg expected the others to honor that command. They would kill him after the runt died, but he would take a few of them with him, for War Claw retained enough poison for at least three more kills.

"But, suh! What about the rat? We can't just leave him!" A tall, lean mouse stepped farther out of line.

"Collins!"

Kreeg laughed out loud. "Leave the general alone, the mousey says." He pointed War Claw at the runt, who now lay shaking on the tunnel floor. "Meaning, no doubt, that I am to be escorted safely to the surface."

He laughed again, feigning confidence. The fools wouldn't honor the runt's next-to-last command.

Would they?

"But, suh?" a mouse said. "Why?"

As Kreeg watched, two mice stumbled forward into the tunnel and knelt.

The runt's eyes stared up at him. In the instant their eyes met, Kreeg understood the terrible truth. Cold fear washed over him.

The scratch in Kreeg's leg. A slow fire burned there. And it was getting hotter.

"Because." The runt coughed. "I have already ... killed him."

Impossible!

Kreeg slumped against the wall of the tunnel. His eyes bulged. His mouth hung open. He looked at the runt for a long time, then stared down at the cut in his leg.

"You?" he asked. He looked at the poisoned claw of his right paw, then shifted his gaze back to the runt, whose words returned in a rush. "*No more trips to the skull jar.*"

Kreeg nodded slowly. "Yes. An empty victory. But then, emptiness always wins in the end, doesn't it?"

"Shut up," someone said.

"Shut up? Why should I? What will you do to me if I don't? You have nothing left, mouse. None of you do. You can't hurt me. ElShua is a lie. His promises are lies. I proved it." He pointed. "That mouse is no king."

FORTY SIX

"SHUT UP!"

Kreeg fell backward and lay crumpled against the base of the tunnel wall. "No king. Just a ... just another mouse."

47
JaRed

JaRed's legs went numb first, then his fingers, wrists, arms. His mouth filled with cotton. His heart somersaulted in his chest.

DeStra knelt beside him and cradled his head, but he couldn't feel her touch. Her eyes filled with fire, as distant as the stars, and as unreachable.

"Don't you do it," she said. "Don't you give up."

JaRed's lungs banged for air, rattling like pistons in a too-fast rhythm. *Hirr-hee, hirr-hee, hirr-hee, hirr-hee, hirr-hee ...*

"JaRed!"

He stared up at her. He tried to move his mouth. Failed. Felt himself falling into numbness. Irresistible weariness settled on him.

"Don't you die!" DeStra squeezed his shoulders. "Do you hear me? Do you hear me!"

He struggled to keep his eyes open. Struggled to

breathe. Struggled to keep the unsteady banging of his heart going one pulse at a time.

"Stay with us. Please. Don't do this to me. Not again. You did it once at the bridge. And I knew then. I did. I knew. I always knew. I lied to you in Kreeg's dungeon. Do you hear me? I lied! I always knew you were meant to be king of Tira-Nor, but I was afraid. And you can't—" DeStra choked.

Heaviness tugged at JaRed's eyes. The world swam in dark waters.

Gibbs appeared in the gray haze, touched DeStra's elbow. "Miss?"

She ignored him. Her voice came from far away. "You can't die now. You can't. You have to be king. JaRed?"

Kreeg's voice clawed the silence. "I see it!" He gasped. "Blackness. A void. I was right. Nothing, after all. I was right. I was ... I ... was ..."

JaRed closed his eyes. Relaxed. Let his lungs empty.

"Miss?" Gibbs's voice was a pinprick in the distance. "It's over."

DeStra began to weep.

Darkness enveloped him.

He heard other voices, soft in the silence, but could not make out the words. But one sentence remained clear in his mind, replaying itself in a litany of bitterness. *You're no king, mousey.*

He fought to keep the words away, but they swarmed through his mind like insects. *You're no king. You're no king. You're no king. You're no king ...*

Madness reached for him with grasping fingers, and JaRed could not move to get away, could not hold his paws to his ears, or shut his eyes, or scream for the insanity to stop. The words of madness invaded his mind.

They were true.

JaRed was no king.

This hurt worse than anything. ElShua had promised. *Promised!*

But that promise had failed.

A chill wind swept over him, freezing the blood in his veins.

Light pierced the black chamber of his vision. Wings like mounds of snow split the awful emptiness. His body jerked, was lifted. Ripped upward, heaving through dirt and stone into open air.

Below him, tree-matted forests fell away to nothing.

The talons that carried him let go without warning, but he did not fall.

He lay on grass in an open field.

A familiar voice found him there. "I've wasted my whole life. I finally tried to do something for others, and it turns out not to have mattered. It won't make any difference. No one even knows."

288

Thunder growled over the blue-hazed mountains in the distance.

JaRed found that he could move again, so he rose to all fours. He peered over the tufted heads of the grass obscuring his vision and stared down into a valley. Fields bloomed before him, furrowed into deep ruts and framed by a silver-shored lake.

Bodies littered the field. They lay twisted on the grass, the lilies, the white sand of a narrow beach. He saw their faces, and blanched. They were both familiar and heart-breaking. Cold and lifeless. Blood dribbled from ghastly wounds. Mouths stretched open. Paws clutched at empty air, motionless.

Blang. KoVeek. MeerQo. JoHanan. Luk and Raz.

One of the bodies moved. It crawled toward the field from the lake. A gash on its thigh trailed a long string of crimson in the sand.

"Stupid," the mouse said. "I've been so stupid."

HaRed. My brother ...

JaRed wanted to run, but the blood and the bodies stopped him. Uncertainty rooted him to the ground.

From the pool a figure arose, bathing the shore with ripples as it broke the surface. When it shook its silver-tipped fur, water cascaded in all directions.

The Badger stood directly behind HaRed and spoke, but JaRed could not make out the words.

Thunder boomed again, and he thought the sky seemed very blue.

A man stepped over him. JaRed had been so intent on watching, on listening, that he didn't hear the footsteps. Or perhaps he couldn't have heard, for the man moved as lightly as a hummingbird.

Shame consumed him, settling on his shoulders and hanging there. He knew who it was, though he saw only His back.

Nearby, HaRed gave a long sigh, and then became very still, a puddle of blood collecting in a black sheet beneath his rust-stained thigh. Water lapped at the shore behind him, as though to lick the wound clean.

"These must be awakened," the man said.

The Badger replied, "There is one more also."

HaRed's eyelids fluttered.

The man reached down and pressed a finger to HaRed's cheek. "HaRed. Open your eyes!"

HaRed did. Bewilderment crept over his face, followed by an army of emotions. Wonder, amazement, disbelief.

Joy.

JaRed looked away.

He stood alone now, an awkward distance from his brother, amazed at his own jealousy, his own sense of irritation.

Far away, on the opposite side of the lake, the ground awoke. The soil giggled and hiccuped. It trembled like the shoulders of a kit at a surprise party.

From distant fields mice crowded to the earthen

center of the valley, flowing down from the high places toward the lake.

JaRed felt very much out of place. This party was not meant for him. In a few moments the thousands of mice from the high country would close around HaRed and the others in a vast embrace, everyone speaking at once, their voices like water running over smooth stones.

They were coming for HaRed. For the others.

But not for me.

In the field near the shore the bodies came slowly to life, as though waking from a long enchantment.

This was not what he expected. But did he have a right to expect anything?

Yes.

He had a right to expect ElShua's promises to come true.

He had a right to be made king!

But, no.

"You're no king, mousey!"

In the center of the field two kits stood transfixed, gazing up at the man with wide-open eyes.

"Oh," Raz said in a small, fierce voice. "It's *you.*"

"You, *sir*," Luk said.

The man smiled. "Young heroes. You have made me very proud."

The warrior kits exchanged amazed glances.

"Proud?" Luk said. "But sir, we failed."

"Luk and Raz, sons of KlyMor and ZaReeba. Listen to me. I was with you in the end, though you didn't know it. I saw your courage in the shadows of the Great Hall. I saw you stand together in the darkness when the rats overcame you and the grown-ups who should have been your defenders fled in terror. What you did was not failure. It was victory. For no one ever fails by resisting evil. But now I must ask you to do something even more difficult. Would you make me doubly proud?"

"Sir," Raz said, "I would do anything for you."

"It will take great courage, and you will suffer much in the years ahead. Everyone there does."

"But mother will have joy again," Luk said.

"Yes."

JaRed backed away and put his head down.

The voice of thunder rolled again from behind him, swelling in his ears. "Where are you going?"

It occurred to him that the question was directed at him, so he turned back.

The man stood with his back erect, gazing at JaRed with his head cocked to one side.

JaRed started to say something polite. Something respectful. Instead, words spat from his mouth in a bitter torrent. "You told me I would be king. You promised."

"Who do you think you are?"

A rebuke.

JaRed's face flushed. He felt small and misunderstood. He felt angry, too, like a child unfairly punished. His head hurt. His heart hurt. Perhaps he shouldn't speak this way. But Kreeg's words still burned in his soul, and he didn't know how to extinguish them.

He wanted to hide, to get away. He wanted to say something that would allow him to sneak off into the wild wood, something familiar and dismissive.

Never mind, he tried to say. Instead, other words exploded from him. "It isn't fair! You promised!"

Silence.

Underneath and behind his own misery, the joy of HaRed's homecoming grew. The universe was aware only of its own blind happiness. The only person who knew of JaRed's torment was the one who had caused it.

"JaRed ... Who do you think you are?"

Slowly, he began to weep.

I'm just me. A commoner. But other words tumbled out. "You promised. Promised! But it never happened. I don't understand that. And maybe I don't need to understand. But then, if your words can't be trusted ..."

Tears streamed down his face. He tried to stop them at first, then surrendered to the torrent.

The man's voice fell on him like a spring rain, mixing with his tears. It brushed the carpet of grass and blew across his face. "What is a king, JaRed?"

"A king," JaRed said, "is supposed to act like a king."

"Yes."

"A king is supposed to be the one who protects his people."

"Yes."

"The one who serves them!"

"Yes."

"Even when—" His words stopped. No more would come. He stared in silence.

"The true king is the one who sacrifices himself for his people." In two strides the man towered above JaRed. "The one who loves them." He lowered himself. Pressed his face close to JaRed's own. He reached out with one finger and stroked the back of JaRed's neck, trailing warmth.

A shock, a vibration, a current flooded his body.

Loves them?

JaRed turned his head.

"You have been a good king, JaRed son of ReDemec."

The man's eyes dazzled in their brilliance, shining with the same light JaRed had seen in the Badger.

All at once he understood what that light was. The light of the eyes. The heart of the Badger. The flame that kindled the fire in the garden forge.

The one thing stronger than death.

JaRed shut his eyes.

Love.

"You have been a good king. But your work isn't finished."

48

JaRed

JaRed's chest filled with air, his lungs expanding like a bellows. He opened his eyes.

Gibbs blinked. His jaw dropped.

Someone drew a sharp breath.

"Suh ..." Private Collins whispered.

DeStra let out a startled sob. Her pretty face was streaked with tears. Her paws were clasped together, as though she held something tiny and fragile. Her eyes widened. "JaRed?"

He sighed and reached for her. "So. You lied to me? In Kreeg's dungeon?"

"JaRed!"

"You know, you mustn't ... you mustn't lie ... to your king."

EPILOGUE
Runt the King

S oon after the battle with Kreeg, JaRed sent for the outlanders in the chapel above the wall. They didn't need to scavenge the North Meadows during the coming summer. Tira-Nor welcomed them as full citizens, for they had strong backs and willing hearts.

But the outlanders did not come. One after another, JaRed's messengers returned alone. Three times the offer was refused.

"Did you make the offer clear?" he asked the last messenger.

"Yes, majesty. But only one mouse answers. The fat one they call Bigums."

"I see."

JaRed felt oddly misunderstood. *Perhaps they will respect me. I will go to them in person.*

On a brilliant spring morning, he and Gibbs swept

up the pollen-flecked steps of the chapel and into the rainbow light of the altar. Without waiting for permission, JaRed repeated his offer. He spoke directly to the outlanders, looking each of them in the eye as he paced the carpeted floor. He offered them hope and a future, asking only their allegiance to him as the king of Tira-Nor.

A long silence followed.

At last Bigums rose and kicked a great pile of shredded newspaper into the air. A chunk of rotting corn struck the front of a pew and thudded on the carpet. "Allegiance? That's a laugh! Why should we trade our freedom for your stupid kingdom? We're our own masters here. We have no king. We need no king!"

The bits of paper he kicked upward settled slowly to the ground around him like flakes of ash.

"But you do have a king," Gibbs said. "He is king whether you accept him or not. He is Lord of the Known Lands whether you believe it or not. And because he is king—and not some other—you might live well in his lands even while you deny him. But you will be missing out on the real thing. The real laughter of the feasts of the Great Hall. The real joy of the festivals of Tira-Nor. You will be stuck with nothing more than this." He waved a paw at the mounded debris, the blackening corn husks and paper bags and strings of plastic wrapping. "An unworthy kingdom. And the illusion of freedom."

Bigums' face paled to an unearthly white. His lips quivered with rage. Before he could speak, a high-pitched, humble voice chirped from the shadows under the pews. "I'll come."

"Me too."

"And me."

One by one, dozens of outlanders stepped forward into the light of the stained-glass window. Several smiled, though nothing particularly funny had been said.

When Bigums finally found his voice, over forty of them stood with JaRed. It was clear the others would remain in the chapel.

"Get out!" Bigums shouted. "Get out get out get out! Who needs you? Every mouse for himself. Go bow down to the little impostor if you want. Suits us fine. More for the rest of us. We'll see who laughs last. Ha ha ha!"

But Bigums' face burned red, and his voice carried no mirth whatsoever.

───※───

If many in the Families resented JaRed's offer to the outlanders, they liked his other changes even less. New connecting tunnels were dug between the Commons and the Families. The old system of commoners belonging to the king was eradicated. From now on, the mice of the city would be taxed, not enslaved.

Advancement would be earned, not purchased.

Colonel Gibbs and the Grenadiers remained in Tira-Nor. Songs were sung in their honor, and the legends of their deeds—which hardly exaggerated the reality—became so numerous that the word Grenadier became synonymous with adventurer. At play time, children went grenadiering, and spoke in surprisingly accurate accents. They held their backs straight like posts, and saluted with the palms of their paws, and poked out their tongues, and challenged to duels any adults unfortunate enough to be designated a play-time rat.

Gibbs, whenever he came across such a game, screwed on his sternest, most disapproving face, clapped both paws behind his back and scowled mournfully. "Grenadiers. Is that any way to approach an enemy? I am most surprised. You must know the code of conduct for a Grenadier is quite clear? But did I see some of my Grenadiers sticking out their tongues at the enemy? Appallingly bad manners. Not to mention unwise. For what if you were to sustain a sudden blow to the back? What then? A shorter tongue, I should think. No, the proper way for a Grenadier to insult an enemy is to thumb one's nose. Like this."

———✤———

JaRed married DeStra WilloWind, and together they

raised eleven orphans in the years following that terrible winter. Among these was the son of Captain Blang and KahEesha.

JaRed often took little Norrie on his knee, told him stories of the courage of his parents, or of the grand heritage of Tira-Nor that was his through birthright. Sometimes JaRed even spoke about Norrie's name and what it meant. Norrie was, of course, a slang derivative of the mouse word for promise.

But he rarely mentioned the one thing that made the lad really stand out, the thing at which adults gaped in awe.

For the boy's own good, JaRed simply ignored it. He knew what it was like to be different. What it was like to ache just to be normal. To wish the weight of the world wasn't hanging on you alone.

Norrie's fur was white as milk.

JaRed son of ReDemec the Red lived long as king of Tira-Nor. Under his reign the city prospered and became both fat and powerful.

In JaRed's later seasons, a crest of snowy fur marched down his spine, following the path of ElShua's fingertip almost to his waist. He was known as a wise and just ruler, renown for the visions and revelations that came unexpectedly through his lips.

It is true that as Tira-Nor prospered, some of the

younger generation tended to scoff at the idea of ElShua, and sometimes JaRed's dreams were troubled by visions of terrible destruction and horror, of Cadrid and the slave trade.

Eventually, long after the other warriors of his generation passed from old age to renewal in the Garden Beyond, JaRed found himself so full of years that he sometimes wished he had not outlived the friends of his youth.

One evening he slipped out into the warm summer air alone. He could still move without being seen, though not without the pain and aches of old age. But this night he felt spectacularly well. And he wanted to take a little air without a bunch of nattering fuss-budgets from the kingsguard tagging along, asking him if he was quite up to a long journey, and if he was warm enough, and if he thought he might die at any moment.

He slipped past the guards at the Royal Gate as though they were blind to his passing, and padded through sighing grass to the edge of the Dark Forest. Overhead, the moon blazed full and somber in the night sky, and stars sailed the black sea of the heavens like distant ships.

He did not know how far he went before the heavy mist descended around him. He felt no fear. Which was odd, because what he sought on this night had been the thing he feared most for many years. But now he felt only anticipation.

To his surprise, the Badger rose up in front of him and stood in a pool of silver light. Vast power coursed through his limbs. "What would you ask of me?"

JaRed drew himself up, his back straight, and took a deep breath. "Why did you kill so many of the kingsguard?"

"Is that all?"

JaRed hesitated, then said, "Why did you spare me?"

A long sigh. A voice like steam rolling through the heavens. "The answer to both questions is the same. It was mercy."

"Mercy? But they died."

The Badger rose on two legs, its front paws hanging down. The great burning eyes pierced the mist. "Death is not always terrible."

"Ah," JaRed said. All at once he understood why he felt so well, why the guards had not seen him, why his steps whispered on the grass.

Then the gentle, velvety smooth talons of the Great Owl closed around his body.

This time the transition was seamless, like waking from a very long and dark dream into a sunlit field on the first day of summer, and JaRed heard the laughter of a thousand mice bounding toward him over an open plain.

Runt the Hunted

is the second book in a series that began with the award-winning *Runt the Brave*. Daniel Schwabauer is currently working on a third novel about the mice of Tira-Nor, *The Curse of the Seer*. For more information and for updates on the series, visit:

www.clearwaterpress.com

RuHof
Cav
Tall Grass
Tira-N
Dry Gully
Round Top
The Dar
Forest
To West
Exiter
Win
Cli
White River
TyMin's Path